A Field Guide • Volume III

Sha

MW01089370

Poplarware

Merry Post

A Field Guide • Volume III

Shaker Baskets & Poplarware

By Gerrie Kennedy
Galen Beale
Jim Johnson

Photographs by Paul Rocheleau

Berkshire House

Stockbridge,
Massachusetts

SHAKER BASKETS AND POPLARWARE:
A Field Guide, Volume III
Copyright © 1992 by Berkshire House Publishers.
All photographs © 1992 by Paul Rocheleau. All rights
reserved. No portion of this book may be reproduced –
mechanically, electronically, or by any other means,
including photocopying – without written permission
of the publisher. For information address Berkshire
House Publishers, Box 297, Stockbridge, MA 01262.

Library of Congress Cataloging-in-Publication Data

Kennedy, Gerrie. 1953-
     Shaker baskets and poplarware: a field guide/by
Gerrie Kennedy, Galen Beale, Jim Johnson: photographs by
Paul Rocheleau.

     p.   cm. – (Field guides to collecting Shaker antiques,
ISSN 1053-136X; 3)
     Includes bibliographical references and indexes.
     ISBN 0-936399-21-x: $12.95
     1. Baskets, Shaker   I. Beale, Galen, 1942-   .
     II. Johnson, Jim, 1941-   . III. Title. IV. Series.
     NK3649.5K46   1992
     746.41'2'088288 — dc20   92-25855
                                    CIP

ISSN 1053-136X
ISBN 0-936399-21-x

Printed in the United States of America

10 9 8 7 6 5 4 3 2 1

"All work done, or things made in the Church for their own use ought to be faithfully and well done, but plain and without superfluity. All things ought to be made according to their order and use; and all things kept decent and in good order according to their order and use. All things made for sale ought to be well done, and suitable for their use."

Father Joseph Meacham
First American-born leader of the Shaker Society
(1741-1796)

Contents

A Note on the Shakers

The Shakers—or the United Society of Believers in Christ's Second Appearing, as they called themselves—began their history in Manchester, England in the mid-18th century. An illiterate factory worker named Ann Lee, born in 1736, became the leader of the sect.

In 1774, she and eight followers set sail for America, where they believed they could live a more holy life, free from the persecution they experienced in England, and with the hope of establishing a new way of life for themselves and their followers.

Arriving in New York, they eventually traveled north on the Hudson River and settled at Niskayuna, which was also called Watervliet, a few miles from Albany, New York. With her small band of followers, she prepared for converts. She died in 1784, several years before the first Shaker village was established.

In the 1790s, the number of converts began to grow dramatically. By 1800, eleven communities had been formed in New England. In the first years of the 19th century, the Shakers pushed westward and established a community in Pleasant Hill, Kentucky, in 1806. Shortly after, other communities were formed in Kentucky, Ohio, and Indiana.

By 1840, there were eighteen communities in existence and the Shaker population peaked at approximately 4,000 to 6,000. Following the Civil War, their numbers began to diminish and reached approximately 1,000 by the end of the century. Beginning with the closing of the community in Tyringham, Massachusetts, in 1875, the communities began to dwindle. Today only one survives—Sabbathday Lake, Maine.

Shaker belief was practiced in communities where members devoted themselves to work and worship. Believers, as they called themselves, were organized in families of celibate brothers and sisters.

Life within the community was quietly busy. Large communal Families of celibate Brothers and Sisters shared responsibilities equally but worked and slept in separate quarters. There were special houses for children, brought into the community with their families or as charitable wards. Following Mother Ann's dictum, "Put your hands to work and your hearts to God," the society spent every day but the Sabbath at work.

Their main business was raising food and providing daily necessities for family members. But they were also craftsmen in a wide range of trades: carpentry, cabinetmaking, black-smithing, spinning and coopering, to name a few. Shaker craftsmen and craftswomen incorporated their principles into their work: durability, simplicity, utility, perfection, grace. Their religion fostered excellence in temporal as well as spir-itual matters. The Shakers recognized talent as a gift from God and believed themselves entrusted to develop their abilities to the highest degree.

Living in community also affected Shaker work. Communal life freed individual members from the economic pressures experienced by craftsmen in the world. In such an atmos-phere the finest work was expected and accomplished.

Because of the fine craftsmanship and durability of Shaker goods, the number of customers for Shaker-made products in the 19th century was large. Among the most popular of the products made and sold by the Shakers were a wide variety of baskets and poplarware, which they sold to the World's People.

While the number of Shakers has diminished to fewer than a dozen, interest in their crafts continues to grow. What makes Shaker craftsmanship exceptional is the passion for excellence and the emphasis on simplicity. The work of the Shakers continues to be admired and respected. The objects they made represent the essence of Shaker life: utility combined with simple grace. In the objects they made, their spirit and standards for perfection of workmanship live on.

Introduction

There are several reasons to write a book about Shaker baskets and poplarware.

There are few concise or practical guides for Shaker baskets, aimed at helping people identify and evaluate true Shaker examples.

To date the Shaker poplarware industry has only briefly been examined in print, primarily focusing on how it was made. This book covers the 100-year history of the craft as it progressed from village to village.

Our knowledge about these crafts evolves constantly through study, research, and a popular revival of these crafts. It's important to us that we share this experience with students and collectors.

Most important of all, study of the baskets and poplarware in this book—and all those that didn't make it into this volume —enables people to read the language of these crafts in a way that fosters a better understanding of Shaker history, daily life, work, and industry.

By delving into the historical record more deeply than is typical in many field guides, it's our hope that the commentary will help the reader better understand the complex linkages that relate Shaker baskets to those made by the Northeast American Indians and the European settlers of New England.

Although basketmaking started earlier, the crafts of making baskets and poplarware overlapped, and were done concurrently by the Shakers at many villages. As the Sisters worked to create new income sources, there were transitional containers, many with palm leaf, which was first woven like the ash baskets, then on a loom, like the poplar cloth. While poplarware is not basketry, the two crafts do have significant similarities.

Both ash baskets and poplarware are made from native woods and were completely processed by the Shakers in their communities.

Both woods are woven, the ash with itself, the poplar on a loom with cotton thread.

While the men of the communities did the heavy work involving cutting the trees and processing them in the mills, the majority of the work of the basket and poplarware industries was carried out by the Sisters.

Both the later baskets and the poplarware found a ready market in the world, and were designed and sold in a manner calculated to attract business, and create additional income for the villages.

Both crafts were strongly influenced by the Victorian age.

The white color of the wood was greatly valued in both crafts, often necessitating bleaching the ash.

Both were shaped on molds, the baskets to a much greater degree.

The Shakers produced similar products from both materials, such as pincushions and fitted sewing baskets.

Twenty or thirty years ago, examples of basketry and poplarware were not hard to find. The diligent collector could set down the road from any of the Shaker villages and expect to discover one or two examples in nearby antique shops.

Yard sales were another rich source, particularly in regions close to Shaker villages. When the Shakers closed their villages, for examples, their neighbors frequently purchased their remaining crafts, implements, and furniture. Spring cleaning sometimes yielded several authentic examples. It still does.

Auctions were another common source. At one auction in Northfield, Massachusetts, we found on top of a mahogany bow-front chest of drawers a perfect Shaker orchard basket—a basket that made the fancy chest of drawers look plain by comparison. And the basket sold for a fraction of what a Shaker basket commands today.

Although poplarware items are now actively sought in the marketplace, affordable pieces are still available. Auction prices for poplar have been rising dramatically in recent years, with rarer pieces selling for thousands of dollars. However, small poplar boxes can still be found on the market today for under $100.

This field guide is divided into two parts: Shaker baskets and poplarware. The basket portion is organized largely by the function of the basket, without particular emphasis on the community of manufacture. The poplarware portion, on the other hand, is organized by community of manufacture. Why? The text will explain why it's relatively easy to accurately pinpoint the "birthplace" of Shaker poplarware; and why it is an often difficult enterprise in the case of Shaker baskets.

This leads to the issue of selection. How do you choose a limited number of examples to represent the wide range of types and styles, and the purposes for which these containers were designed and used?

We started by limiting our selection of baskets largely to museum collections. There are fine examples of almost every type of Shaker basket in the collections of the major Shaker museums. The basket and tool collection at The Shaker Museum, Old Chatham, New York, is particularly bountiful and fine.

The poplarware chosen for this book includes examples of the most common forms produced by the Shakers. These are the boxes that were sold in the greatest volume in the village stores, on road trips, and through catalog sales. Consequently these are the boxes most likely to be found today. Paul Rocheleau's detailed black and white photographs illustrate the finer points of construction that point to the community of origin, and help date a piece. The color plates beautifully illustrate these pieces of Shaker Victoriana, and show why they were loved by the World and Shakers alike for their exuberance, color, and intricate craftsmanship.

In making the final selection of baskets from museum collections, our emphasis has been on the aesthetic value of the basket. When confronted with a choice, we intentionally selected examples that appealed to our sense of design and proportion.

But we were equally concerned with the who, what, when, where, and why of our selections. In many cases, the finest example was put aside in favor of a basket that could be associated with a particular Shaker community, or about which other important information is known.

We also selected examples that had some interesting or unique feature—in one case, for example, setting aside a perfect example for the sake of showing a similar, but lesser, basket with repairs in its handle.

We are grateful to these Shaker musuems for their assistance: Hancock Shaker Village in Pittsfield, Massachusetts; The Shaker Museum in Old Chatham, New York; Lower Shaker Village Museum in Enfield, New Hampshire; The Fruitlands Museum in Harvard, Massachusetts; The New York State Museum in Albany, New York; The Shaker Heritage Society in Colonie, New York; The United Society of Shakers at Sabbathday Lake, Maine; and Canterbury Village, Inc., Canterbury, New Hampshire.

A special acknowledgment is due Frederick Miller, a member of the New York bar and a volunteer basketmaker at the Hancock Shaker Museum. Fred generously contributed his research, editorial, and interpretive talents to this project of Shaker history and basketry.

We are equally grateful as well to the following individuals whose knowledge, experience, and friendship over many years has inspired and greatly assisted us in our work: Mary Rose Boswell, Rita Braskie, Diane Conroy-LaCivita, Richard and Roberta Dabrowski, Kenelm Doak, Magda Gabor-Hotchkiss, Roger and Marge Gibbs, Jerry Grant, Douglas Hamel, Eldress Bertha Lindsay, Stephen Miller, Elizabeth Shaver, June Sprigg, Maggie Stier, Jim and Nola Stokes, and Eldress Gertrude Soule.

Color
Plates

1. Rectangular Basket

Probably Mount Lebanon, NY

A black-ash utility basket. Inscriptions on tag: "Things to be whitened in Spring when the weather permits." "1941. Christmas cards of every [illegible]. Some new ones, some that have been answered, and some that were not answered. Emma J. Neale."

Height: 8½"
Length: 17½"
Width: 12⅞"

The Shaker Museum,
Old Chatham, NY
585

2. Kittenhead Baskets

Watervliet, NY

*Delicate examples of Shaker "fancy work"
ornamented with a pincushion, a sawtooth
inner rim, teardrop shaped handles, and two
bands of cranberry-colored splint.*

(Left)
Height: 2½"
Diameter: 3¾"
Overall Height: 5½"

(Right)
Height: 2⅛"
Diameter: 4"
Overall Height: 3⅛"

*The Shaker Heritage
Society, Colonie, NY
SHS 031; SHS 570*

3. Silk Top Basket

New York or New England

*A Shaker fancy work version of a Victorian
sewing purse imported from Asia.*

Height: 1"
Diameter: 3"
Overall Height: 5"

*Fruitlands Museum,
Harvard, MA
1028.1987*

4. Twilled Baskets and Mat

Mount Lebanon, NY

Fancy work reflected in basket bottoms and table mats. The twilled-weaving pattern is sometimes called quatrefoil or "quadrifoil" by modern collectors.

Largest Diameter: 11″
Smallest Diameter: 4¾″

The Shaker Museum,
Old Chatham, NY
and Fruitlands Museum
Harvard, MA
370.1979; 356; 3180;
370.1979; 14338

5. Lidded Knife Basket

Mount Lebanon, NY

A choice example of a Shaker "knife" basket, another popular design of the "fancy work" era. This basket is described on page 73.

Height: 4⅞″
Length: 11½″
Width: 8¼″
Overall Height: 9⅞″

Hancock Shaker Village, Pittsfield, MA
62-181 B

6. Orchard Basket

Mount Lebanon, NY

*This is a Mount Lebanon, New York,
Orchard Basket. They were ordinarily used
to gather fruit for both indoor and outdoor
use. To see a similar example, turn to page 53.*

Height: 16"
Diameter: 15¼"
Overall Height: 13½"

*Hancock Shaker Village,
Hancock, MA*
76-47.3

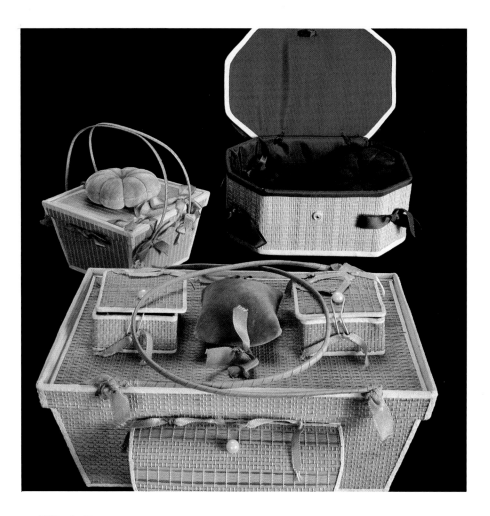

7. Work Boxes

(Top left)	(Front)	(Top right)
Square Work Box	*Work Casket*	*Ladies' Work Basket*
Church Family,	*Alfred, ME*	*Canterbury, NH*
Mount Lebanon, NY		
	Late 19th century	*Mid-20th century*
Late 19th - early 20th century		
	Height: 4¼"	*Height: 2⅞"*
Height: 4¼"	*Length: 7"*	*Length: 7¼"*
Base: 3¼" square	*Width: 4"*	*Width: 4⅝"*
Private Collection	*Private Collection*	*Private Collection*

These examples are described on page 132.

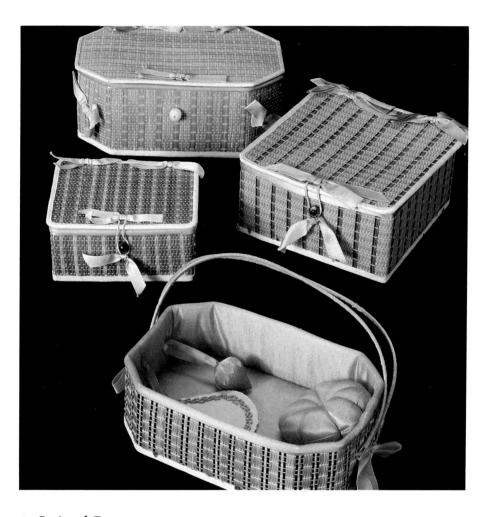

8. Striped Boxes

(Top)
*Work Box , Possibly
Canterbury, NH*
*Height: 2¾",
Length: 7¼",
Width: 4⅝"*
*Late 19th century,
Private Collection*

(Center left)
*Handkerchief Box ,
Community
unknown*
*Height: 1⅞",
Length: 4¼",
Width: 3⅜"*
*20th century,
Private Collection*

(Center right)
*Handkerchief Box,
Community
unknown*
*Height: 2¾"
Base: 5½" square*
*20th century,
Private Collection*

(Bottom)
*Open Work Box ,
Community
unknown*
*Height: 2",
Length: 6¼",
Width: 3"*
*Early 20th century,
Private collection*

These examples are described on page 133.

Shaker Baskets & Poplarware

CHAPTER

1

❧ Baskets

Utility Baskets

Transitional Baskets

Fancy Work Baskets

Tools for Basketmaking

The Development of Shaker Basket Styles

There are only two distinct styles of Shaker baskets: the utility basket, and the so-called "fancy work" basket.

Early Shaker utility baskets appear tough and rustic, at least when compared to later Shaker styles. But function, not form, was the early basketmaker's concern: basic container-ship in an agricultural community. Refinement would come later as Shaker basketmakers perfected their prototypes.

It's probable that the Shaker brethren began to make baskets when those available from the Native Americans failed to meet specific community needs. Native American baskets were frequently made from lightweight splint, and were not, as a result, especially durable. By way of contrast, early Shaker baskets were hefty working implements for home use: in the Believers' fields, orchards, barns, and workrooms. But they were also being sold to the public as early as 1809.

The Shakers first employed the manufacturing processes of the Northeast Indians. Characteristically, however, they soon began adapting available technology to better their efficiency, production levels, and the quality of their product.

One example involves the preparation of woodsplint, which the Shakers called "basket stuff." Instead of repeatedly pounding logs manually with wooden mallets, they adapted for this laborious task the mechanical trip-hammer, a black-smith's tool.

Early basket handles and rims were carved by hand and shaped with drawknives and files. Later, mechanical saws and routers were used to refine and standardize shapes. The Shakers also fabricated wooden molds to guarantee perfectly formed baskets, uniform in size, volume and shape.

These improvements in basic technology would ultimately result in the mass production of unique basketware for the World's People, and a lasting worldwide reputation for their simple grace and excellence.

The manufacture and sale of basketware was a joint interest for both sexes in the community. This would change, however, when the male population began to decline significantly in the mid-19th century. With that decline, responsibility for the industry would pass to the Shaker women.

This shift of burden, economic and functional, would also feminize the design of Shaker basketware. Another important influence on the craft was the tastes of Victorian tourists for "fancy goods" on their visits to the resorts and spas of New York State and New England and nearby Shaker villages. A third phenomenon occurred with the emergence of factory basketmaking: the production of inferior but inexpensive baskets and adequate substitutes.

These were formidable influences. Combined, they would effectively end the commercial manufacture of utility baskets by the Believers. But the Shaker women persevered and adapted. The upshot was a new commercial product for the World's People: the "fancy work" basket.

Delicate crafts produced by the Shaker sisters were frequently called "fancy goods." This is not a Shaker term, but a Victorian concept for novelty items, like trinkets and souvenirs. The fact remains, however, that Shaker basketmaking reached its peak in overstuffed Victorian America, both in the level of production, and in the highly stylized baskets that were manufactured especially for that market.

The Importance of Mount Lebanon Baskets

While the historical record is not complete, it's likely that baskets were made at most of the Shaker communities. These were, after all, frugal and agricultural communities. So there's no reason why baskets would not be made for personal and community use, if not for sale to the public.

But numerous Shaker records do survive, and they make clear that basketmaking thrived and excelled at the Mount Lebanon community. Indeed, the basketmakers of the Church Family at Mount Lebanon produced the great paradigms of all Shaker basketry, wherever made.

One reason for Mount Lebanon's success rests in the fact that two generations of Shakerdom's highest leaders, both male and female, were committed basketmakers. The influence wielded by these "patrons" of the craft insured that this industry was firmly supported by the entire Shaker community, and that its work product measured up to exacting quality standards.

Basketmaking began with the manufacture of utility baskets, principally for "home use" within the community. But in the 1830s, the Church Family basketmakers at Mount Lebanon, under the leadership of Elder Daniel Boler (1804-1892), transformed this craft into a mass-production industry, a 60-year venture that produced, by one reliable estimate, as many as 70,000 baskets.

A large part of that effort is recorded in a Memorandum of Baskets, an annual journal maintained by the Church Family basketmakers from 1855 to 1874. Its pages capture a unique glimpse of the industry at its busiest, and during its decline toward the end of the 19th century.

Basketmaking at Mount Lebanon was seasonal work from autumn through spring, with a continuing corps of ten to fourteen Shaker sisters assigned to the weaving of baskets. They produced an average of 3000 baskets each year—a prodigious work product even with 10-hour work days.

From 1855 through 1867, their production levels increased annually, with a record 3866 finished baskets by the spring of 1867. Then production began to decline, beginning with 1000 fewer baskets in 1868, followed by several hundred fewer baskets each year thereafter.

The heavy hand of illness and a scarcity of experienced weavers is apparent. As one sister poignantly observed, "A continual change of experienced help for the young and insufficient is no great advantage to this business. The winter past there has been more constant failures in the shop occasioned by sickness than I have ever known for 20 years."

This decline in production by the second—and last—generation of Shaker basketmakers parallels, in fact, the decline within Shaker society itself. Older members were dying, "backsliders" were leaving to join the World's People, and smaller numbers were converting to their austere faith.

The final blow to the industry fell with a disastrous fire at Mount Lebanon in January 1875. The conflagration destroyed numerous buildings of the Church Family. The loss included an inventory of baskets, tools and molds, and raw materials. Attempts were made to revive the industry, but with scant success. Annual production levels after 1875 were counted in the hundreds, never thousands.

Being the center of basket manufacture, Mount Lebanon produced the greatest number, and the finest-made, of Shaker fancy work baskets. There's far less documentation of basket-making in commercial scale at other Shaker communities. Many Shaker records have been lost or destroyed. A Memorandum of Baskets is the most complete, notwithstanding it covers only 19 years of an industry that spanned a century of Shaker history. At best, perhaps, the picture will always be incomplete.

❧ Baskets

Utility Baskets

Transitional Baskets

Fancy Work Baskets

Tools for Basketmaking

9. Three Work Baskets

Early utility work baskets likely manufactured at the Church Family basket shops at Mount Lebanon. Each has a square flat bottom, and is made from heavy black ash splint.

a. Painted inscriptions
Basket (left): The initials "B.S." Basket (rear): "1," with the initial "G" underneath. Basket (front): "2."

b. Handles
Double-grip handles, notched to hold the basket rims securely, permitted two people to share the carrying burden. Also, utility baskets with double-grip handles could be stored in stacks.

Probably Mount Lebanon, NY

(Left)
Height: 19½"
Diameter: 26½"

(Rear)
Height: 15"
Diameter: 23"

(Front)
Height: 11¼"
Width: 22 ½"
Length: 23 ¼"

The Shaker Museum,
Old Chatham, NY
681; 3666; 3665

10. Large Rectangular Basket

Probably Mount Lebanon, NY

Height: 12¼"
Length: 36½"
Width: 15½"
Overall Height: 14½"

The Shaker Museum,
Old Chatham, NY
8238

The bottom of this black ash utility basket was woven with a "filled," rather than "open" weaving pattern, to prevent the spillage of its contents. The basket's unusual proportions suggests that it was made for a specific use within the community, now unknown.

As Shaker communities closed, their properties were frequently sold, or were transferred to surviving Shaker villages. This makes the exact identification of a Shaker basket's site of manufacture difficult, even for museum curators.

This basket was one of several obtained from the Shaker community at Hancock, Massachusetts. After the death of Hancock's last Trustee in 1957, Eldress Emma B. King of the Central Ministry at Canterbury undertook to close the community, liquidate its properties, and arrange for the care of its three remaining Sisters.

a. Painted inscription
"ELDs. N. F. 1866," a probable reference to the Elders of the North Family at Mount Lebanon.

11. Rectangular Work Basket

This is the earliest dated basket in a
Shaker collection, and the work of an
inexperienced basketmaker. It was
woven without the use of a mold from
black ash splint, which was first
scraped to produce a smooth exterior
finish. Three hardwood cleats on the
underside of the basket establish
utilitarian function in the community.

a. Painted inscription on handle
"D. 2 1829."

b. Rims
Here, basic and hand-carved, but their
half-round profile would evolve into a
standard feature of Mount Lebanon
basketware. The single lashing on the
rims was begun by anchoring the
lashing splint to the outside body of
the basket. Later Shaker lashing
techniques would conceal this beginning on the inside of the basket, or
between the rims.

Like the preceding Rectangular Work
Basket, this basket was obtained from
the Hancock Inventory in 1957.

Probably Mount Lebanon, NY

Height: 10½"
Width: 15"
Length: 25½"

The Shaker Museum,
Old Chatham, NY
8866

12. Rectangular Work Basket

This black ash utility basket, woven on a wooden mold, is an excellent example of mid 19th-century basketware from the Church Family basketshops at Mount Lebanon. The skillfully formed bonnet-shaped handle and the half-round profile of its rims are standard design elements in the best of Mount Lebanon baskets.

a. Inscription on tag
"This basket belongs to Office Brethrens' Room for Clothes. Return."

b. Handle and rims
The handle is notched for the outside rim, but its maker cut the notches too deeply into the handle stock. As a result, the handle split above each rim. The later tinwork, fastened with copper tacks, is a subtly effective repair effort. This basket was obtained from the Hancock Inventory in 1957.

Probably Mount Lebanon, NY

Height: 9⅜"
Width: 17⅛"
Length: 21¾"
Overall Height: 16"

The Shaker Museum,
Old Chatham, NY
600

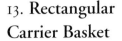

13. Rectangular Carrier Basket

This carrier basket, in near-perfect condition, is one of the best surviving examples of the quality of craftsmanship achieved by the Church Family basketmakers at Mount Lebanon.

Narrow black ash split, scraped to a sheen finish, was used for both the vertical spokes and horizontal weavers. The bottom has a "filled" weaving pattern, and is reinforced with three maple skids fastened with copper tacks.

The carrier's bonnet-shaped handle and half-round rims clearly distinguish it as a Mount Lebanon basket. At each corner, the basketmaker has reinforced the rims with copper tacks before double-lashing them.

The rounded interior surface of the handle, tapered slightly above the rims, is a functional accommodation to the human sense of touch. But the form that follows this function adds a special note of grace to the whole effect.

This carrier was obtained from the Hancock Inventory in 1957.

Probably Mount Lebanon, NY

Height: 7¾"
Width: 16¼"
Length: 21¼"
Overall Height: 16"

The Shaker Museum,
Old Chatham, NY
8516

14. Basket Handles and Rims

The handles and rims on these two utility baskets help identify their communities of manufacture. The basket on the left has a gracefully proportioned bonnet-shaped handle, half-round rims, and a double lashing, all hallmarks of Mount Lebanon basketware.

Design features of the basket on the right suggest a Canterbury origin. The handle is flat and squat. The rims are more angular in shape than those manufactured at Mount Lebanon, and they are lashed together with a single lashing.

Probably Mount Lebanon and Canterbury

The Shaker Museum, Old Chatham, NY 8516; 65-279

15. Handle and Rim

The photographs on this spread highlight identifying features of Mount Lebanon baskets. Note, first of all, the interior round shape of handle and rim, with faint traces of file markings. The handle is notched to accept the inside basket rim. The "leg" of the handle is tapered, and inserted into rows of horizontal weavers. As in this basket, the Church Family basketmakers used lightweight splint for the lashing of their basket rims.

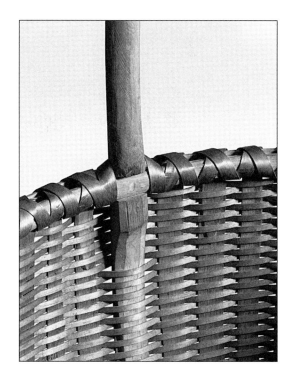

Mount Lebanon, NY

Hancock Shaker Village,
Pittsfield, MA
73-98-4

16. Rectangular Work Basket with Lining

A large collection of baskets survives at the Canterbury community. But despite an ample recorded historical record of that Shaker community, there is scant primary evidence that basketmaking was a significant industry there. In fact, many baskets in the Canterbury collection may be the result of Canterbury being the recipient of the assets of other Shaker communities when they closed.

a. Lining
This black ash utility basket is lined with blue ticking (striped blue on white) that has been stitched to the rims. This basket design is frequently called a "chip basket"; that is, a carrier for wood chips and other kindling. Wooden skids are frequently attached to the bottom of these carriers to promote strength and durability.

b. Handle and rims
This carrier lacks the polish and sophistication found in Mount Lebanon basketware, particularly in its squat handle and angular-shaped rims. Here, the basketmaker's principal concern was clearly function, not aesthetics. Harmony in design has also been sacrificed by the use of wide vertical spokes and narrow horizontal weavers.

Probably Canterbury, NH

Height: 10¼"
Width: 15¼"
Length: 20"
Overall Height: 15½"

The Shaker Museum,
Old Chatham, NY
6347

17. Rectangular Work Basket

a. Handle and rims
This black ash utility work basket
features a length-wise handle, an
accommodation to human comfort in
carrying the basket and its contents.
The hand-carved handle is also typical
of Canterbury basketware. And its
rims are angular, unlike the half-round
profiles produced by the Mount
Lebanon basketmakers.

Probably Canterbury, NH

Height: 10"
Width: 15"
Length: 25"
Overall Height: 21"

Hancock Shaker Village,
Pittsfield, MA
65-279

18. Two Round Baskets

Canterbury's large collection of round baskets includes many that were made from white ash, rather than the black ash that the Mount Lebanon basketmakers favored. White ash is readily available and easy to harvest, but its splint is more brittle and difficult to use than black ash splint.

Again, squat handles, angular-shaped rims singly lashed, wide vertical spokes, and narrow horizontal weavers are distinctive features of Canterbury basketware. Note also that this basketmaker turned the top of every other vertical spoke down into the exterior weavers. Mount Lebanon basketmakers usually reversed that process to conceal these construction details.

a. Penciled inscriptions on bottom left "S.I." "S.C. Heath" and "I.B.H."

Probably Canterbury, NH

(Left)
Height: 8¾"
Diameter: 11¼"
Overall Height: 13"

(Right)
Height: 10⅝"
Diameter: 15¼"
Overall Height: 16¾"

The Shaker Museum,
Old Chatham, NY
16,135; 6349

19. Round Basket

This example, woven from white ash splint, is similar in construction to the baskets in the preceding photograph. The fineness of its splint suggests that it was intended for indoor household use.

a. Inscription engraved in handles: "1". This designation may refer to a room in a Shaker building where the basket was assigned, or the basket's volume.

Probably New Hampshire or Maine

Height: 12½"
Diameter: 17⅛"
Overall Height: 14½"

The Shaker Museum, Old Chatham, NY
6911

20. Two Round Baskets

The tub-shaped utility basket (left) is woven from black ash splint; and its neighbor from white ash splint. Both have double grip handles mounted to the outside of the basket. One has singly lashed rims; the other, a double lashing. Both are fine examples of round Canterbury field baskets.

Probably Canterbury, NH

(Left)
Height: 8¾"
Diameter: 13¾"

(Right)
Height: 10¾"
Diameter: 15¾"

The Shaker Museum,
Old Chatham, NY
6348; 6852

21. Two Round Baskets

Typical baskets in the collection of the Sabbathday Lake community. Although the Maine communities—at Gorham, Alfred, and Sabbathday Lake—made baskets, the craft never approached the scale of basketmaking at Mount Lebanon.

Maine utility baskets reflect the influence of Native American basketmakers, and the work of rural basketmakers. In fact, many of these Shaker products, in the company of Native American and farm baskets, would be difficult to distinguish as being Shaker-made.

Maine baskets lack a uniformity in manufacture. There is little consistency in their shapes, or in their handles and rims. Utility baskets were woven without molds, and their handles were usually hand-carved. Because production levels in these small rural Maine communities remained modest throughout their history, it's understandable that their baskets did not achieve the quality of craftsmanship so evident in the Mount Lebanon product.

The reinforced bottom is a common design element in Maine basketware, influenced by the basketware of local Native Americans. Reinforcement protects the bottom from damage through use, and strengthens the basket's structure. It also elevates the basket from the ground. It is achieved by weaving a coil of lightweight splint to the underside of the basket; or by lashing a piece of heavy splint, of pencil-like thickness, to the bottom.

a. Handles and rims
The grip handles and basket rims are hand-carved. Some lashing has been replaced on both baskets.

b. Bottoms
Both baskets have a pencil-thick piece of splint lashed to the bottom.

c. Finish
The basket (front) has a finish of red paint.

(Back)
Height: 14⅜"
Diameter: 23¾"
Overall Height: 16½"

The Shaker Museum,
Old Chatham, NY
7244

(Front)
Height: 10¾"
Diameter: 20¼"
Overall Height: 12¼"

Sabbathday Lake, ME
5222

22. Round Basket

Although this basket was obtained from the Canterbury community in 1958, it is more typical of Maine basketware.

a. Inscriptions
"Office" is painted on both handles. The bottom is inscribed, "E. Canterbury, N.H. Office."

b. Bottom
Round bottom with pencil-thick splint lashed to bottom.

c. Rims
Similar to Native American construction; heavyweight splint with beveled edges.

d. Handles
Hardwood with a minimum of tooling evident.

Probably New Hampshire or Maine

Height: 11"
Diameter: 21"
Overall Height: 13"

The Shaker Museum, Old Chatham, NY 10686

*Probably New York
or New England*

*Height: 10½"
Diameter: 14½"
Overall Height: 16½"*

*Hancock Shaker Village,
Pittsfield, MA
61-125*

23. Round Basket with Leather Lining

This early Shaker utility basket shows signs of heavy use and wear. The lining indicates that the basket was probably designed and manufactured for farm and garden use.

a. Handle
Roughly tooled with a minimum of scraping, but nonetheless symmetrical. The handle fits on the outside of the basket body.

b. Bottom
Round bottom with braided splint lashed to the bottom as a skid.

c. Spokes and weavers
Unusually wide spokes tapered toward basket bottom. Weavers are of heavyweight splint, but with a satin finish.

d. Lining
Leather lining is stitched under the basket rim.

24. Work Basket with Lining

A beautiful example of Mount
Lebanon craftsmanship, woven from a
square bottom to a round top. These
baskets are frequently called "apple
baskets," but they had multiple uses in
a Shaker community, indoors and out.
Indeed, the leather lining in this basket
indicates that this example was
intended for farm use other than the
gathering of fruit or its storage.

Mount Lebanon, NY

Height: 9¼"
Diameter: 14½"
Overall Height: 14"

The Shaker Museum,
Old Chatham, NY
44

a. Inscriptions
Painted on handle: "E.P.W." "C.V.H."
"58" [1858].

b. Handle
A typical bonnet-shaped handle from
the Mount Lebanon community. It is
finely carved, filed, and scraped to a
smooth finish. The handle's width
narrows as it approaches the rims.

c. Lining
Leather pieces stitched together. A
strip of canvas-like cloth is glued to
the top of the lining and
around the rim.

d. Bottom
The bottom, on each
side and across the
center, is reinforced
with hand-carved hard-
wood cleats fastened with
copper tacks.

25. Orchard Basket

Mount Lebanon, NY

Height: 8¾"
Diameter: 14½"
Overall Height: 15½"

Private Collection

Another example of the classic Mount Lebanon orchard basket. Its present condition attests to many years of heavy use.

a. Inscription
Painted on handle: "OMT."

b. Bottom
Square bottom reinforced with three hardwood cleats fastened with iron tacks.

The initials "OMT" are those of Orange Maria (Moriah) Treadway, a one-time Deaconess and Eldress of the South and Church Families at the Watervliet community. Born in 1810, Moriah entered the community in 1823. The Watervliet journals record that Sister Moriah peddled bonnets on sales trips to the World's People, cultivated silkworms, and cared for her ailing sister Almira, who was also a Shaker.

26. Chase Weaving

Near perfect symmetry and balance in plaited basketry is best achieved by weaving with an even number of vertical spokes. One weaving technique popular with the Shakers is called a "chase" weave. It begins by bending a tapered horizontal weaver around one of the vertical spokes. This produces "two" weavers, connected at the bend. The two weavers then "chase" one another as the weaving proceeds.

In this basket, the chase weave begins with the fifth spoke from the left. Most Shaker fancy work baskets, but not all, incorporate this chase weave.

Probably New England

Private Collection

27. Body of Basket

This photograph demonstrates how Shaker basketmakers typically created an odd number of vertical spokes: by dividing a single vertical spoke in two. Plaited basketry generally employs an odd number of vertical spokes.

This weaving technique is not, however, uniquely Shaker. It is commonly found in Northeast American Indian splint basketware. But in fancy work baskets, the Shakers preferred to weave with an even number of vertical spokes, in order to produce baskets having a more precise balance and symmetry.

Mount Lebanon, NY

Hancock Shaker Village, Pittsfield, MA
73-98-4

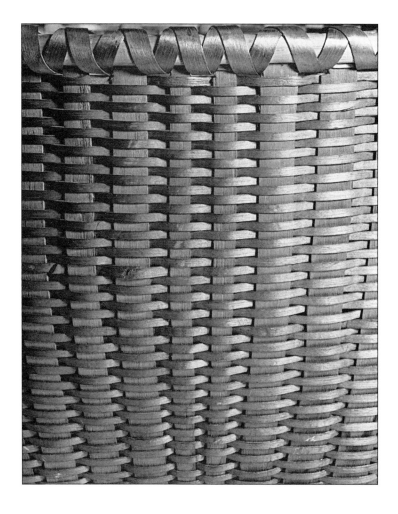

❧ Baskets

28. Household Basket

This example represents a transition in Shaker basketmaking; from the utility basket to the fancy work. The horizontal weavers on this substantial household basket are made of light-weight splint, 3/32 inches wide. The handle and rim are equally delicate: only 3/16 inches wide.

This basket was obtained from the Hancock Inventory in 1957. There are five similar examples in the Hancock Shaker Village museum collection.

a. Handle
One is missing.

b. Condition
Broken vertical spokes and horizontal weavers throughout. The splint used in these transitional examples is too delicate for the overall size of the baskets. As a result, only a few original examples survive, none of which is in good condition.

Hancock, MA
or Mount Lebanon, NY

Height: 5"
Diameter: 12½"
Overall Heights: 6¾"

The Shaker Museum,
Old Chatham, NY
8960

29. Twilled Basket Bottom

Hancock, MA
or Mount Lebanon, NY

Hancock Shaker Museum,
Pittsfield, MA
75-154

The bottom of a transitional basket. The twill or herringbone weave pattern produced the "filled" bottom, a weaving pattern commonly found in Shaker sewing baskets.

The satin-like exterior finish of the vertical spokes and horizontal weavers is another characteristic of Shaker fancy work basketry. The sheen is achieved by simply exposing the interior grain of black ash splint. In its natural state, the interior grain of black ash has the surface texture of satin ribbon. From this is derived the Shaker basket term "satin," to describe the quality of processed splint.

30. Cathead Basket

Another transitional basket, not quite utilitarian and not yet Shaker "fancy." This medium-size basket was intended for household use. It is lightweight and airy. Inverted, the shape of the basket resembles the profile of a cat's head. This is the source of its popular name—"cathead." Smaller versions are called "kittenheads."

a. Handle and rims
Carved bonnet-shaped handle. The rim is made from a black ash annual growth ring, ¼ inches wide. Regrettably, the use of lightweight splint in this basket provided inadequate support for the handle. As a result, it has lost its original symmetrical shape.

b. Bottom
In the interests of mass production, most Shaker fancy work baskets have an "open" bottom. The open bottom required the consumption of less raw material, and was faster to execute than a twill or herringbone pattern.

Probably Mount Lebanon, NY

Height: 5½"
Diameter: 7"
Overall Height: 9½"

The Shaker Museum,
Old Chatham, NY
43

31. Cloth-Covered Knife Basket

A choice example of a "knife" basket, which the Shakers manufactured and sold in a variety of sizes. We can only speculate at the origins of the names used by the Shakers for their baskets, such as "knife," "spoon," and "saucer," but earlier versions of these containers could have been utilitarian, and used for the storage of kitchen utensils.

a. Handle and rims
Lightweight and delicate. The handle bows outward at the center due to the basketmaker's use of a lightweight rim, which is inadequate to maintain the handle's shape.

b. Lining
A type of waterproof oil-cloth, light tan in color with a brown floral design. The lining, inside and out, is carefully pieced and sewn together, and glued to the body of the basket.

c. Weavers
Through a tear in the lining, delicate $\frac{1}{16}$ inch-wide weavers are evident. They are nearly white in color, as the lining has protected them from exposure to sunlight and air.

Probably Mt. Lebanon, NY

Height: 4⅞"
Length: 11½"
Width: 8¼"
Overall Height: 9⅞"

The Shaker Museum,
Old Chatham, NY
5567

❧ Baskets

Shaker Fancy Work Baskets

As this Field Guide demonstrates, Shaker basketmaking during the 19th century was an evolving craft. Its earliest products were the firm utility baskets from the workshops of the Shaker Brethren. These were followed by smaller household baskets made by the Sisters: medium-sized baskets designed to hold sewing items, yarn, and the like. They were constructed of lightweight woodsplint, with horizontal weavers frequently as narrow as $\frac{1}{16}$ inches wide. The handles and rims they fabricated were similarly narrow and almost fragile in appearance.

This evolution led to even smaller and more delicate basket-ware, the so-called "fancy work" produced by the sisters for the Victorian marketplace in America. These fancy work baskets proclaim a feminine hand at work. The Sisters were no strangers to meticulous handwork such as sewing, stitching, and the weaving of silk thread. These skills they adapted to the technology of miniaturization and fine basketry.

While the ornamentation on these Victorian novelties may seem out-of-step with traditional Shaker notions of simplicity, the fact remains that the Shaker fancy goods shops existed to appeal to public consumers, and produce needed income for their then-declining communities. Moreover, many of the ornaments used on these baskets could be justified as being functional: ribbons to attach handles, for example, and colorful emeries to sharpen sewing needles.

For many collectors, Victorian fancy basketware is wood-splint basketry at its finest. The sisters imposed a remarkable fineness on a rough and stubborn hardwood. Woodsplint basketry simply can't get much finer than that constructed of splint only $\frac{1}{32}$ inches in width.

32. Three Knife Baskets

Three more examples of Shaker "knife" baskets. They exhibit a range in size, as well as a fineness of construction, common to Shaker fancy work. Knife baskets were popular basketware products for the World's People, and the Shakers produced large numbers of them.

a. Penciled inscriptions
(Rear) "Laura Prentess" [1809-1882]. (A member of the Watervliet community.)

(Front) "Sr. Phoebe Van Houten" [1817-1895] (A member of the Mount Lebanon community.)

Watervliet and Mount Lebanon, NY

(Rear)
Height: 4¾"
Length: 12"
Width: 7½"
Overall Height: 9"

Shaker Heritage Society, Colonie, NY
SHS 061

(Left)
Height: 5"
Length: 12½"
Width: 8¼"
Overall Height: 10"

Private Collection

(Right)
Height: 4½"
Length: 6"
Width: 4½"
Overall Height: 7"

The Shaker Museum, Old Chatham, NY
11730

33. Kittenhead Basket

The kittenhead is a smaller version of the Shaker cathead basket. Shaker Sisters manufactured thousands of these popular novelty baskets, but being only novelties and souvenirs, their owners did not ascribe high values to them. As a result, relatively few original examples survive.

a. Handles
Two tear-drop handles made of black ash growth ring. One handle has been replaced.

b. Rims
Beveled black ash growth ring.

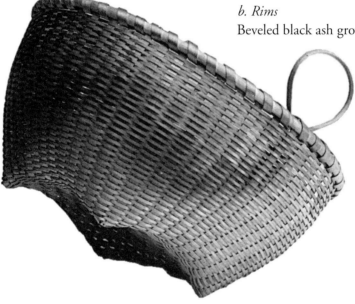

New York or New England

Height: 5¾"
Diameter: 6¾"
Overall Height: 7"

Fruitlands Museum,
Harvard, MA
FM 380

34. Two Rectangular Baskets

The miniature (left) was made of black ash splint with a sawtooth rim. It is in near-perfect condition. It was woven from delicate weavers $\frac{1}{32}$ inches wide. It was obtained from Polly Bruce, the daughter of a former member of the Watervliet community. It was made by Sister Mary Dahm, a leading basket-maker at the Watervliet community, and later at the Mount Lebanon and Hancock communities, where she remained until the closing in 1959.

The basket (right) is an adaptation of the Shaker "knife" basket, and was likely intended for light household use, such as sewing.

a. Penciled inscription
"2 Ea" on bottom.

b. Damage
Minor damage to lashing where the rim stock overlaps.

Watervliet, NY
and Massachusetts

(Left)
Height: 1"
Length: 2¼"
Width: 1⅝"

The Shaker Museum,
Old Chatham, NY
17,728

(Right)
Height: 1¾"
Length: 6½"
Width: 4½"
Overall Height: 2½"

Fruitlands Museum,
Harvard, MA
FM 379

35. Knife Basket with Twill Cover

A skillfully woven example of fancy work constructed of the finest black ash splint. Most of these baskets were sold as "covered" or "uncovered," a Shaker reference to "lids." Many basket lids incorporated twills and hexagonal weaving patterns. Few examples of these delicate baskets survive.

a. Rims
Lightweight beveled growth ring.

b. Handle
Age has distorted the original symmetry of the handle.

c. Lids
Both lids are woven in a twill pattern and finished with a sawtooth edge. The lids are hinged at the center of the basket, and attached to a wooden stretcher with copper wire.

d. Bottom
A filled bottom, with fine black ash splint.

New York or Massachusetts

Height: 4⅞"
Width: 8¼"
Length: 11½"
Overall Height: 9⅞"

Hancock Shaker Village, Pittsfield, MA
62-181B

36. Cylinder Basket with Twill Bottom

The bottom of this basket incorporates a weaving pattern that the Shakers marketed to the World's People as "twilled." Modern collectors frequently use the terms quatrefoil or "quadrifoil" to describe the four-leaf effect produced by the weaving pattern.

The most common basket forms were "twilled tubs" and "twilled saucers," but the weaving pattern was also used in the manufacture of a variety of fancy hand goods, such as table mats and fans.

This Shaker twill pattern was influenced by, if not copied from, woven products imported from Asia during the Victorian Age in the United States. Another example is the silk top basket.

This complicated and beautiful weaving pattern is difficult and slow to execute. Although there are faster and less "superfluous" ways to produce baskets with round bottoms, the twill was intended to appeal to Victorian consumers who were enthusiastic basket collectors.

a. Bottom
Unusual open-weave center. Most twilled baskets have tightly woven centers.

b. Lid
This cylinder basket had a lid, now badly damaged, with a matching twill pattern. The lid slipped over the open top of the basket.

c. Materials
Black ash splint; vertical spokes $\frac{1}{16}$ inches wide; horizontal weavers $\frac{1}{32}$ inches wide.

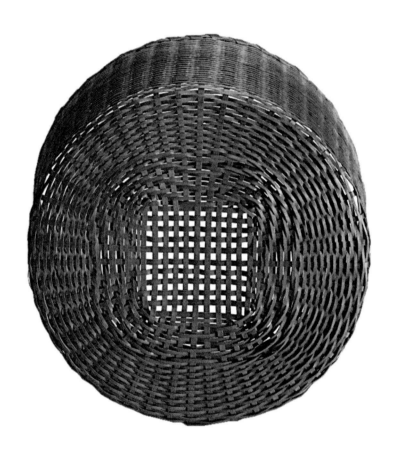

New York or Massachusetts

Height: 2½"
Diameter: 4¾"

Fruitlands Museum,
Harvard, MA
1215.1987

37. Hexagon Weave Baskets

Each of these Shaker fancy work baskets incorporates a hexagonal weaving pattern. These baskets were made and sold as souvenirs for the World's People. They were woven over wooden molds and made of black ash splint, or from palm leaf imported from Cuba. The same hexagonal weave pattern was used in the construction of large straining baskets (popularly called "Shaker Cheese Baskets") for use in the dairy industry.

The two small baskets in the foreground are woven of black ash and feature rims make of kidskin. They were frequently made for sewing work stands, like the one described on page 100.

The example in the rear is made of palm leaf. These baskets were usually attached to the interior of sewing carriers and baskets, and used to hold sewing notions.

The larger round baskets are also made of palm leaf. The uncovered round basket was made by Sister Mary Dahm [1889-1965] while a member of the Hancock community.

Mount. Lebanon, NY, and Hancock, MA

(Rear Left)
Height: 1³⁄₁₆"
Length: 4⅛"
Width: 2⅛"

(Rear Right)
Height: 2"
Diameter: 3½"

(Middle Right)
Height: 1¾"
Width: 3⅜"
Length: 4½"

(Front)
Heights: 1¼"
Diameters: 2"

(Middle Left)
Height: 2½"
Diameter: 3⁹⁄₁₆"
Lid Height: 1"
Lid Diameter: 3³⁄₁₆"

The Shaker Museum, Old Chatham, NY
359; 10,600; 8,359; 4473; 360; 8,937

1

❧ Baskets

38. Wooden Basket Molds

Most Shaker baskets were woven over solid wooden molds. These molds facilitated the mass production of baskets with uniform shapes, sizes, and volumes. They were essential to the development of the Shaker fancy work basket industry and its precise basketware. Because few people outside Shaker communities appreciated their function, few genuine Shaker molds survive outside museum collections.

The round tub molds range in size from 5½ inches to 9½ inches in diameter. They were used in weaving "twilled" baskets. As with all baskets constructed on molds, the weaving begins with the bottom of the basket. The bottom is tacked to the smaller base surface of the mold, and the basketmaker proceeds to weave the vertical sides of the basket.

An interlocking, or collapsible, mold was used to produce a basket with a top opening that was smaller in size than the full width or length of the basket. The interlocking mold (right) was used to make a Shaker cathead basket. Assembled, the mold produces a basket with a height of 4¾ inches, and a center diameter of 5 inches. Once the basketmaker completed the weaving of the body of the basket, the center piece of the mold was withdrawn, and then each of its remaining pieces. If the mold could not "collapse" in this way, the basket could not be removed from the mold.

New York or Massachusetts

The Shaker Museum,
Old Chatham, NY
2436; 3438; 2439; 10,620

39. Handle Forms

In addition to wooden molds for shaping baskets, the Shakers devised wooden forms to precisely shape and bend the handles and rims for their fancy work basketware.

In the early years of the craft, handles and rims were carved from green—or unseasoned—hardwood and shaped by hand. Later, handles would be machine-routed, steam-bent, and dried over wooden forms, as the ones pictured here. Once dried, the handles would retain the shape of their molds.

These molds produced handles ranging in size from 2⅜ inches to 1½ inches wide.

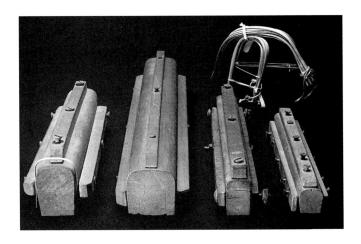

New York or Massachusetts

The Shaker Museum,
Old Chatham, NY
4115-8; 4115-9; 4115-7; 4115-6

40. Basketmaking Tools

The wood planer (rear) was devised and used to scrape black ash splint. It has a metal blade secured in place under a wooden roller. The thumbscrews on top permitted precise scraping adjustments, depending upon the thickness of the basketmaker's splint.

The three hand-held "cutters" (front) were used to prepare narrow widths of splint for fancy work baskets. The "cutters" contain sharp metal blades spaced to exact widths. They were used to cut straw, poplar, and ash. Lengths of lightweight splint were pulled through these blades in the widths required for particular baskets. As in the case of wooden molds, the fabrication of "cutters" was an essential step in the development of a productive and profitable fancy work basket industry.

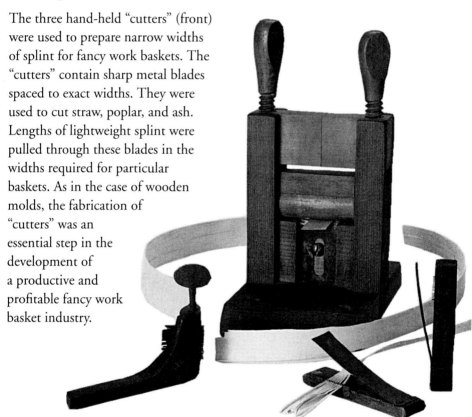

New York or Massachusetts

Hancock Shaker Village, Pittsfield, MA
72.31.2; 59; 62.148

Private Collection

41. Basket Handles and Gauge

This gauge was designed to measure handle stock to standard and precise lengths. In the mass production of fancy work baskets, the Shakers assigned a number to each basket size, and a corresponding number to its matching handle. This gauge was used to produce seven handles of varying lengths, from 4⅝ inches to 7½ inches.

a. Penciled inscriptions
(Front): "Length of Ears April 10, 1870."
(Reverse): "Length of Ears 1868 on the other Side gives Length". (The word "ears" is a Shaker basketmaking term for the shape of a basket handle.)

These ear handles were part of a group of 318 obtained from Sister Mary Dahm, the last basketmaker at the Hancock community.

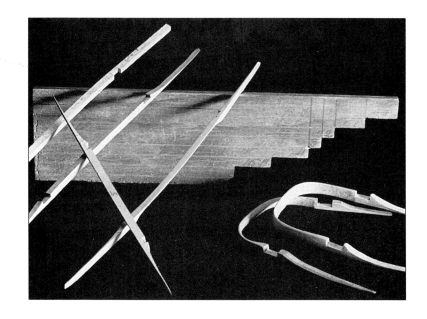

Hancock, MA

The Shaker Museum,
Old Chatham, NY
X87.1; 10,609AS

2

❧ Poplarware

Mount Lebanon, NY

*Sabbathday Lake and
Alfred, ME*

Canterbury and Enfield, NH

Assorted Poplarware

The Shaker Poplarware Industry

The development and growth of the poplarware industry is an excellent example of Shaker ingenuity, craftmanship, and community industry. And, unlike most products of Shaker manufacture, which were also made in the World and often require close examination for accurate authentication, poplarware was produced solely by the Shakers

This unique poplarware industry also illustrates the Shakers' ability to adapt to changes both in their own communities and in the World. Combining their skills as basketmakers, weavers, and sewers, the Sisters were continually experimented with new sales products as their role of income producers rose in the communities. Initially, the Mount Lebanon, New York, Shakers wove and braided rye and oat straw, ash, and palm leaf into a variety of products such as hats, fans, and tablemats. By 1855 they were weaving strips of these materials on looms warped with cotton thread, and by the end of the decade had added "popple" or poplar wood to their range of raw materials. By the 1860s, these Mount Lebanon Sisters were weaving large quantities of both palm leaf and poplar into a cloth that was then fashioned into a variety of fancy boxes that were marketed to the World. With the advent of the Civil War, palm leaf became difficult to import, and poplar became an increasingly important material.

Poplarware represents a successful blending of the Shakers' values of simplicity and craftsmanship and their commercial acumen. During the Victorian era, the Shakers consciously incorporated style and taste trends of the period in the design of their fancy work. Their boxes were lined with colorful

fabrics and decorated with ribbons. Sewing had become a
pleasant pastime, and many poplarware boxes were designed
to hold sewing accessories. Poplar items bore such names as
Veil Box, Card Tray, and Ladies Cuff and Collar Holder,
reflecting the Shaker's awareness of their worldly market. By
the end of the 19th century, the Sister's fancy work industry
had become an important source of income for the villages,
and the poplar items one of the most successful products.

At first glance, poplarware seems quite different from typical
Shaker designs. A close look at the construction of these
boxes, however, reveals the Shakers' continuing adherence to
simplicity combined with high standards of workmanship.
Poplar cloth was made by a joint effort of the Brothers and
Sisters. In the winter, the Brothers selected the straightest
poplar trees, cut them into logs and took them to their mill,
where they were sawed into two-foot lengths. These were
further split into two-inch-square sticks. Because the wood
was frozen, each stick could be shaved into paper-thin strips
with a vertical plane; the resulting curled shavings were
collected in a basket. The Sisters removed and straightened
the strips by finger pressing, laying them on racks to dry in a
heated building. After drying, the strips of wood were re-wet,
split with a specially fashioned spliting gauge into $\frac{1}{16}$th-inch
wide "weavers," and spread out to dry again.

The poplar was woven on a loom warped with #30 white
cotton sewing thread. Various patterns were made on the
loom by alternating the poplar and the white cotton thread.

The Sisters also experimented with color and design by incorporating different weaving materials into the poplar cloth, including natural and dyed sweet grass, ash, and straw. When the cloth was cut from the loom, white paper was pasted to the reverse side to give the cloth additional strength. As the last step in production, the cloth was cut into pieces ready to be fashioned into boxes.

The Sisters made all the poplar boxes in the winter, finishing them in time for their spring cleaning and garden planting. Boxes were made either by gluing the poplar cloth to a wooden form, or by sewing fabric and batting to a strip of poplar-covered cardboard and nailing this strip around a wooden base. Lids and accessories were fastened with ribbons, giving the boxes a festive look.

The World did not take up this craft, probably because the manufacture of poplar cloth was seen as too labor intensive. For the Shakers, who already had saw mills, wood planes, and looms in place, it was a natural fit, and the Shakers' communal lifestyle enabled them to easily mass produce these containers.

By the 1860s, the village stores were well stocked with poplarware products for the growing numbers of sightseers who visited these villages. The Shakers also agressively marketed their poplarware in other ways, selling it at fairs, by catalog, and on extensive sales trips. These Sisters and Brothers were continuing a long tradition of selling on the road. Their sales trips took them the length of the east coast, with stops at most of the grand hotels of New England, and forays to resorts as far south as Florida. To further widen their markets, they published catalogs in which they listed their Fancy Goods—brushes, boxes, cloaks, sweaters, and poplarware.

Poplarware production reached its peak at the beginning of the 20th century and continued until the 1960s. The villages of Mount Lebanon, New York, Sabbathday Lake and Alfred, Maine, and Canterbury, New Hampshire, were the largest producers of poplarware, and the villages of Enfield, New Hampshire, and Hancock, Massachusetts, are also known to have made limited amounts of poplarware.

The poplarware illustrated on the following pages represents the finest examples of the most common boxes made by the Shakers. The names of the boxes are taken from Shakers' catalogs, and because they are handmade, the dimensions, while accurate for the individual piece, may vary slightly for other pieces of the same type. We hope you will be as delighted as we are by the products of this craft, which are pure Victoriana and uniquely Shaker.

CHAPTER

2

❧ Poplarware

Mount Lebanon, NY

Sabbathday Lake and
  Alfred, ME

Canterbury and Enfield, NH

Assorted Poplarware

42. Octagon

This classic fitted octagonal work box is well suited to illustrate the descriptive terms that will be used throughout this chapter. The four "fittings" that were customarily stored inside poplar work boxes are shown for display purposes on top of this box. These fittings—a pincushion, needle book, emery, and wax—were fixed inside by ribbons that extended through the sides and were decoratively tied on the outside of the box.

In addition, features of cloth, weave, ribbon, button, and kidskin will be introduced, since they will be referred to repeatedly.

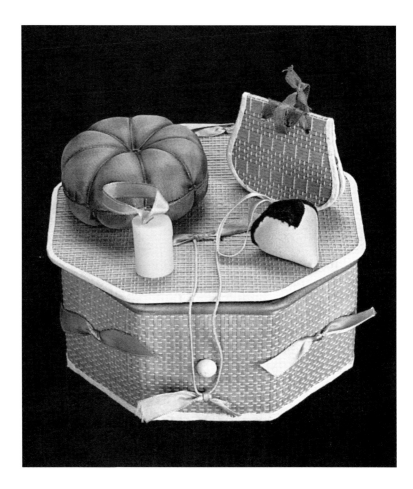

Alfred, ME

Late 19th century

Height: 4¼"
Base: 3¼" square

Woven poplar, pink satin silk, cardboard, cotton batting, paper, rose ribbon, kidskin, copper tacks, shoe button, paper clip, elastic, pine, wallpaper, Alfred stamp

Private Collection

a. Weave
Poplar cloth was woven on a loom warped with cotton thread. Different patterns were achieved by alternating the warp and the weft threads, and these patterns are distinct clues to the origin of the box. Two different weaving patterns can be seen here, one on the box and the other on the needle book.

b. Ribbon
Ribbon was used to hinge the lid to the base of the box, as well as to attach any fittings to the sides of the interior. Because ribbons were tied in a number of ways, varying from community to community—some with loops, some without—the method of ribbon tying can offer further clues to the community that produced the box.

c. Button
There are definite patterns in button types on poplar boxes. The fastener on the front of this box is a shoe button that is attached with a round, nickel-plated paper clip on the inside.

d. Kidskin
The Shakers trimmed the raw edges of their first boxes with heavy paper, but being too fragile, paper was replaced by kidskin.

e. Pincushion
Pincushions, often made with fabric matching the interior, are found in either round or square shapes. They were stuffed with wool and were often embroidered in the "tomato" design seen here.

f. Needle book
Needle books are folded sheets of poplar cloth lined with either fabric or paper, and trimmed with kidskin. Inside, several flannel "leaves," or "pages," with pinked edges are held in place by a ribbon that is tied on the outside of the needle book.

g. Emery
Emeries were filled with emery powder and used to sharpen needles. They were often made in the shape of a strawberry with fabric that matched the inside of the box, and were topped with velvet hulls.

h. Wax

Thread was run across these beeswax cakes to give it added strength and prevent it from twisting and knotting. Made in specialized molds with a looped ribbon attached, the cakes can be found in a variety of shapes. The three most common are a round wax shaped like a tiny Christmas tree ball; a mini cupcake shape; and the cylindrical, tin can shape seen here.

Part of the fun of collecting poplarware is being able to identify the community in which a box was made. Variations from box to box in weave, ribbon, button, and fittings can be helpful in pinpointing individual communities. As the boxes that follow are discussed, you will be able to sharpen your identification skills.

i. Mount Lebanon Stamp

Many poplar boxes were stamped on the base with the community's stamp. This stamp was used on products made by the North Family Shakers, Mount Lebanon, NY.

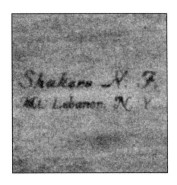

43. Oval Carriers

These two oval carriers, one of woven ash (left), and the other of woven poplar (right), date from the period of the Shakers' transition from the basket industry to the woven poplar cloth trade. They hint at the Shakers' experiments with materials, weaves, and techniques in their ever-evolving craft industries. The techniques used in the construction of these carriers continued into the poplar industry even though this large oval carrier shape did not.

a. Weave
The carrier on the left has a dark wooden cloth exterior made of finely cut brown ash strips woven over each other in a pattern similar to patterns that would later be used for poplar cloth. The simple, flat woven cloth of the carrier on the right was created on a loom using a heavy cotton thread for warp, and strips of poplar for weft. Weaving with a cotton warp was introduced in Shaker communities around 1855, but ash baskets had been made in great numbers long before then. The technical skill revealed in the weave of the ash cloth is much higher than that of the poplar cloth.

b. Handles and rims

The handle of the poplar carrier has been executed with much more flair than that of the ash carrier. The ash carrier handle is beveled on the edges, rounded inside, and flat on top. The two small holes drilled in each side indicate that it was intended to be used for an oval box handle. Here, it is nailed to the rim and shimmed with a piece of metal. Both handles are attached to the inside of the carriers, but the one on the poplar carrier tapers nicely as it approaches the top rim.

These carriers have only interior rims. The interior rim of the ash carrier is covered by the blue fabric lining. The one on the poplar carrier remains uncovered and appears to be in two halves, which are skillfully thinned and joined behind the handle.

b. Lining

The poplar carrier is unfinished, with only a light cloth backing the poplar. The ash carrier is finished with a dark blue fabric lining that is carried to the top of the rim, and wrapped over the wooden interior rim.

c. Leather trim

On both carriers, strips of leather have been used to decoratively cover the raw edges of the cloth. On the ash carrier, plain brown leather has been used to trim the top and bottom edges of the woven ash, and the wide vertical strips used below the handle on either side of the carrier cover the butted edges of the ash cloth. The thinner, white kidskin that became the preferred material in poplar boxes can be seen trimming the edges of the poplar cloth.

d. Base

Both carriers have wooden bases. The exposed pine base of the unfinished poplar carrier shows the pencil markings drawn to mark the placement of the handle. The base of the ash carrier is covered with fabric.

(Left)
Church Family,
Mount Lebanon, NY

Mid-19th century

Height: 12¾"
Length: 20⅝"
Width: 14⅝"

Woven brown ash, leather,
blue homespun fabric, pine,
wooden handle, metal

Private Collection

(Right)
Church Family,
Mount Lebanon, NY

Late 19th century

Height: 10½"
Length: 19⅞"
Width: 13⅞"

Woven poplar, pine, wood
handle, woven cloth covering

Private Collection

44. Oval Work Stand

This Work Stand, which also came in a variety of forms, is a good example of the Shaker's ability to make use of both products and skills used in earlier crafts. The pine top on this stand is adapted from an oval box, and the turned legs are very similar to those used on footed spool stands. A skilled basketmaker produced the small ash basket with the open cheese weave bottom that is seen on the left, and the straw braid frequently used in Shaker bonnets is used to trim the top edge of the Work Stand.

a. Top

The pine top is covered first with green fabric and then again with poplar cloth edged with braided straw. Five sewing accessories are attached to the top: a velvet pincushion; an ash basket trimmed in kidskin; a half-round poplar box with a drawstring green silk top; a flannel covered needle book attached to the side of the box; and at the back, metal pins for spools of thread. A narrow strip of poplar, bound with kidskin, is tacked down on the front edge, allowing spaces perhaps for storing scissors.

b. Drawer

The green cardboard drawer, faced with poplar cloth, is held in place by a strip of poplar shaped over wire that is tacked underneath the oval top. The drawer is lined with printed paper, and underneath the drawer are more strips of paper that appear to have been cut from continuous sheets of ornate awards and incentives given to schoolchildren. These paper strips on the bottom of the drawer read in part: "I have been so faithful to imitate my copy, that I have received two new copies today"; "I have been so naughty and willful, that I have no reward but this - a ticket of disgrace./witness Instru."

Church Family,
Mount Lebanon, NY

Mid- to late 19th century

Height: 2⅝"
Length: 9"
Width: 5⅜"

Woven poplar, straw braid,
green satin silk, green velvet,
ash, printed paper, kidskin,
cardboard, green glass
button, wire, pine, flannel,
metal pins

Private Collection

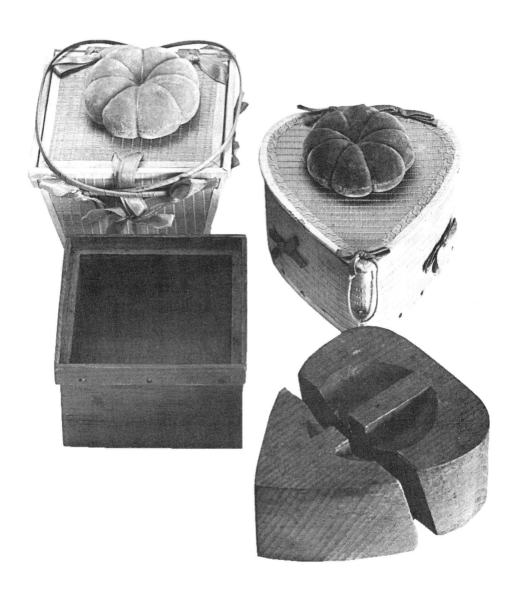

45. Poplar Boxes and Molds

(Left rear)
Square Work Box

*Church Family,
Mount Lebanon,
NY*

*Late 19th century -
early 20th century*

*Height: 4¼"
Base: 3¼" square*

*Woven poplar,
white embossed
paper, yellow rib-
bons, cane, pine
frame. Fitted with
pincushion, emery,
and wax*

Private Collection

(Left front)
*Wooden Form for
Jewel Box*

*Church Family,
Mount Lebanon,
NY*

*Late 19th century -
early 20th century*

*Height: 2¼"
Base: 3⅝" square*

*Pine, copper tacks,
nails*

Private Collection

(Right rear)
Heart

*Church Family,
Mount Lebanon,
NY*

Late 19th century

*Height: 2½"
Length: 4¾"
Width: 4"*

*Woven poplar, rose
ribbons, white em-
bossed paper, pink
patterned paper,
copper tacks, metal
paper clip, elastic,
pine. Fitted with
emery, wax, pin-
cushion*

Private Collection

(Right front)
Heart Mold

*Mount Lebanon,
NY*

Late 19th century

*Height: 2½"
Length: 4¾"
Width: 4"*

Pine

*The Shaker
Museum,
Old Chatham, NY
3561*

As the poplar industry evolved, a variety of composite construction techniques were used to compensate for the poplar cloth's inherently weak structure. Some boxes were made by pasting the poplar cloth on a wooden form as seen in the canted work box (left rear). The plain, straight-sided Jewel Box form (left front), a variation of the Square Work Box, was also covered with poplar cloth. In recent years these box forms have often been misidentified as berry baskets or measures.

Adapting the basketmaker's technique of using molds, complex shapes—such as the Heart—were made by forming poplar covered cardboard strips around a wooden mold, both of which are seen here. These Heart boxes were made by the dozens beginning in the 1870s.

a. Weave

The poplar cloth on both of these boxes is woven in the simple flat weave often used at the Mount Lebanon, New York, community. This Heart box has a quarter-inch-wide poplar band running around the top edge, a decorative touch that is not common in other poplar boxes.

b. Ribbon

The ribbons on both boxes are tied in the double bow style frequently used by the Mount Lebanon community. Ribbons are used on poplar boxes to hinge the lid and to secure the fittings. The Work Box uses a ribbon loop to lift the recessed lid, while the Heart box has an elastic, which is meant to hook over the missing button.

c. Paper Trim

The Shakers' great skill as paper box makers is reflected in these boxes. The interiors, bases, and raw edges of both boxes are covered with paper. The heavy white embossed paper trim is so carefully cut and folded that at first glance it appears to be kidskin. The Heart box has delicate touches of purple paper trim, and on its lid, a strip of patterned purple paper follows the outline of the edge.

d. Forms and Molds

While the Jewel Box form provided the sides and base, and was therefore not removed after completion of the box, the wooden "collapsible" Heart mold was made in two pieces, and was designed to be removed. The precise shape of a Heart box was achieved by forming strips of poplar-covered cardboard around this mold, and tacking the bottom edge to a wooden base.

❧ Poplarware

Mount Lebanon, NY

**Sabbathday Lake and
    Alfred, ME**

Canterbury and Enfield, NH

Assorted Poplarware

46. Three Lidded Poplar Containers

From the time the poplar industry spread to Maine in 1869, until its end in the mid-20th century, the Sabbathday Lake Shakers conducted a profitable business in this fancy work trade. They sold their poplarware in their community store and on sales trips to resorts throughout the White Mountains and along the seacoasts of New Hampshire and Maine, and were known to have published at least four fancy goods catalogs.

Lidded boxes, dominating the Sabbathday Lake Shakers production work, were listed in the catalogs by names such as glove box, handkerchief box, button box, bead box, silk box, and glove case. In Sabbathday Lake's 1910 catalog, the Hexagon Work Box was offered in only one size. The Silk Box carried a price of $.50.

a. Weave
The weaving pattern on these boxes was one commonly used by the Maine and New Hampshire communities. The pattern runs vertically on the sides, and from side to side on the top.

b. Ribbons

Both Maine communities tied their ribbons in a similar manner. The ribbon was knotted without a loop and the ends were cut on an angle. At times, to achieve better proportion, the size or the number of the ribbons on a box was varied. The Hexagon Work Box has ribbons of two sizes: the side and the top ribbons are one-half-inch wide, while the ribbons used for the hinges and the inside fittings are one-quarter-inch wide. Since it is not necessary to use three bows to hinge the lid of the Silk Box, the addition of the third bow could have been a decorative choice of the maker. The ribbon on the front of the lid was strategically placed to cover the holes for the elastic that hooked over the button. The bow at the bottom of the elastic on the Handkerchief Box and Silk Box was called a "fly," and was purely ornamental.

c. Lids

The lids of the boxes from Sabbathday Lake were cut slightly larger than the base of the box, creating a quarter-inch overhang. This was done to prevent the lid from falling into the box.

d. Kidskin

The kidding on the base of these boxes is wider than the kid edging around the lid. This was a community stylistic choice. The quality of the kid workmanship is best on the Hexagon, where it is stretched smoothly and evenly around the sharp corners of the lid.

e. Buttons

Shoe buttons are most commonly found on boxes from the Maine communities. The shank of the button was fastened on the inside of the box with a round metal paper clip. Initially, white shoe buttons were easy to get. When the supply ran out, the Shakers bought black shoe buttons and painted them white.

f. Fittings

While the Silk Box is empty and the Handkerchief Box has only an emery inside, the Hexagon is fully fitted. The poplar needle book inside this box was woven in the flat Mount Lebanon weave, but it is not unusual to find a needle book in a weave different from that of the box. The wax inside the Hexagon is still wrapped in its original paper, indicating that this box has seen little use.

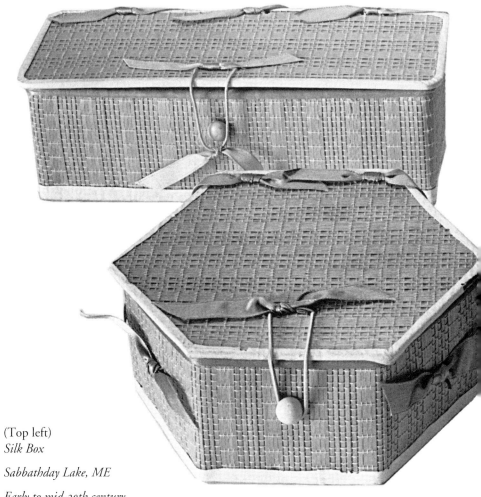

(Top left)
Silk Box

Sabbathday Lake, ME

Early to mid-20th century

Height: 2¼"
Length: 6½"
Width: 2¼"

*Woven poplar, lilac satin
silk, kidskin, lilac ribbon,
shoe button, paper clip,
elastic, pine, tacks, lilac
wallpaper, Sabbathday Lake
stamp*

Private Collection

(Front left)
Hexagon Work Box

Sabbathday Lake, ME

Early to mid-20th century

Height: 2¼"
Width: 4⅜"

*Woven poplar, green satin
silk, kidskin, green ribbon,
shoe button, paper clip,
elastic, pine, tacks, green
wallpaper, Sabbathday Lake
stamp. Fitted with needle
book, pincushion, emery,
and wax*

Private Collection

(Front right)
Handkerchief Box

Sabbathday Lake, ME

Early to mid-20th century

Height: 2¼"
Base: 5¼" square

*Woven poplar, blue satin
silk, kidskin, purple ribbon,
shoe button, paper clip,
elastic, pine, blue wallpaper,
Sabbathday Lake stamp.
Fitted with emery*

Private Collection

47. Jewelry Boxes

Jewelry boxes were a popular sales item, and while sometimes lined with satin silk, the ones from Maine were more often lined with velvet. This Ladies' Jewelry Case was the largest of three sizes listed in Sabbathday Lake's 1910 catalog. As the name Bureau Tray implies, the unlidded box was meant to hold small personal items.

a. Construction
The Jewelry Case is an earlier box than the Bureau Tray. The case's top rim was formed over a piece of wire, which while not visible, can be felt with one's fingers. The technique of sewing the top edge of strips of fabric and cardboard-backed poplar to a piece of wire was an early practice. The wire enabled the poplar strips to be shaped to any configuration. When the desired gauge of wire became unavailable, the top edge of the fabric and cardboard-backed poplar strips were simply sewn right sides together and then reversed.

The interior compartments of both boxes were formed with velvet-covered pieces of wood that were drilled on both ends, and tied to the outside of the box with ribbons. The Jewelry Case is divided into four sections. In the Bureau Tray, the partitions are not parallel.

The back of the Bureau Tray is shown in this photograph to illustrate the joint where the two ends of the poplar strip overlap. It was a widely accepted practice by all communities to locate this joint in the center of the back of the box.

b. Sabbathday Lake Stamp
Devised by Elder Delmer Wilson (1873-1961) for the Sister's fancy goods industries, this stamp was used on most of Sabbathday Lake's products. The "S.C." stands for Shaker Community.

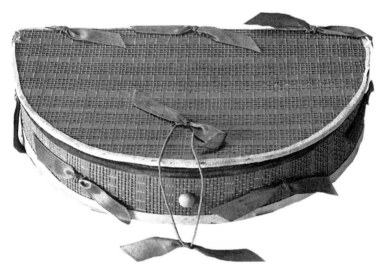

(Top)
Bureau Tray with Compartment

Sabbathday Lake, ME

Early to mid-20th century

Height: 1½"
Length: 9⅜"
Width: 4½"

Woven poplar, red satin silk, red ribbon, kidskin, pine, tacks, white wallpaper, Sabbathday Lake stamp

Private Collection

(Bottom)
Ladies' Jewelry Case

Sabbathday Lake, ME

Late 19th century

Height: 1¾"
Width: 8½"
Depth: 5½"

Woven poplar, blue velvet, purple ribbon, kidskin, wire, shoe button, paper clip, elastic, pine, tacks, wallpaper

Private Collection

48. Work Boxes

(Top)
Work Casket , Alfred, ME

Late 19th century - early
20th *century*

Height: 4¼"
Length: 7"
Width: 4"

*Woven poplar and sweet
grass, pine frame and base,
kidskin, pink ribbon, velvet,
pearl buttons, cane, velvet,
wallpaper. Fitted with
emery, needle book, and
wax*

Private Collection

(Middle)
Bifoid, Alfred, ME

*Late 19th century - early
20th century*

Height: 2"
Length: 7½"
Width: 3½"

*Woven poplar, rose satin
silk, cardboard, pink
ribbon, kidskin, pine, white
wallpaper, Alfred stamp.
Fitted with emery, pin-
cushion, needle book, and
wax*

Private Collection

(Bottom)
Work Casket, Alfred, ME

*Late 19th century - early
20th century*

Height: 2"
Length: 3½"
Width: 2½"

*Woven poplar, pine frame,
white wallpaper, kidskin,
pink ribbon, pink velvet,
Alfred stamp. Fitted with
emery and wax*

Private Collection

The most elaborate poplar boxes came from the Mount Lebanon, New York, and Alfred, Maine, communities. Alfred was situated on land with limited agricultural potential, and early in its history sought other ways of making a living. By 1878 the Alfred Shakers were earning over $1,000 a year selling fancy goods. They sold their products both in the community store and on the road, and as far as known, in 1908 published their only catalog.

a. Weave

The simple, vertical weave on the Bifoid is typical of poplar cloth made by the Alfred Shakers. The same cloth has been used on the larger Casket body, but the poplar strips have been oriented horizontally. The pocket of the large Work Casket incorporates sweet grass strips in another Alfred weave pattern.

b. Shape

The two Work Caskets are very much like the Mount Lebanon boxes with poplar glued to the sides of a wooden frame. The large Work Casket was available in five sizes.

The Bifoid was made by tacking a poplar-covered cardboard strip to a wooden base. The top edge of the Bifoid was formed by sewing the materials onto a wire that was then bent to the serpentine shape. The ends of this box have been partitioned off with fabric-covered cardboard held in place with ribbons. With added lids, two smaller storage containers were created.

c. Handles

The swing handles on the larger Work Casket are wrapped with cane, but this box was also sold with ribbon handles similar to those on the other two boxes. The cane handles are attached to the front and back of the box, and do not readily lie flat when open, a design that hampers the easy opening of the lid.

d. Ribbons

Similar to ribbons on boxes from the Sabbathday Lake community, all these ribbons are tied in knots with no loops. The use of ribbon handles heightens the impression of a riot of ribbons.

e. Bifoid

This box, the smaller of two sold, was called a "Bifoid" in the Alfred catalog, but a similar box in the Sabbathday Lake catalog was listed as a "Biford." The origins of these words are not clear.

f. Fittings

The large Work Casket has two thimble boxes and a pincushion on its lid, as well as a side pocket. The other fittings are attached inside. The smaller Work Casket has room for only a square pincushion on its lid, with an emery and a wax inside. The Bifoid is fully fitted, and the wax is in its original paper.

49. Two Covered Boxes

While most of the poplar fancy work was designed for the needs of Victorian women, several containers were suited for use by men. The half-round shape of the smaller box was used in several villages for jewelry boxes and here, as the catalog name indicates, it was used as a man's stud box. The work box was available in five sizes in the 1908 Alfred catalog. Several of the sizes were sold unlidded as open work boxes.

a. Weave
The dark strips in the cloth of these two boxes are sweet grass. The Alfred Shakers frequently added sweet grass to their poplar cloth, either dying it or using it in its natural color. Introduced in the poplar weave of the Maine communities in 1899, the sweet grass was obtained from the Penobscot Indians in Old Town, Maine. Eventually, however, the Alfred Shakers stopped using sweet grass in their poplar cloth, because they felt it made their work too easily confused with work done by the local Native Americans.

When poplar cloth is pasted to a cardboard backing, the shape of the box determines the horizontal or vertical orientation of the poplar strips. The woven strips must be vertical for the cloth to be readily bent around curves and sharp corners. On poplar boxes with wooden frames, the poplar cloth can be pasted to the wood in either orientation, as seen in the previous boxes.

b. Construction
The Stud Box's early origin is revealed by the technique of forming the top rim over a piece of wire. While not visible, the wire can be easily detected when felt with the fingers.

c. Condition
The minimal wear on these boxes consists of some missing kidskin on the base of the Work Box, and stretched out elastics on both. In time, kidskin becomes brittle and can break off. Copper tacks, used to fasten the poplar cloth to the wooden base, can be seen where the kid is missing.

d. Alfred Stamp

(Left)
Stud Box

Alfred, ME

Early to mid-20th century

Height: 1⅝"
Length: 3¼"
Depth: 2¼"

Woven poplar and sweet grass, blue satin silk, kidskin, blue ribbon, elastic, pearl button, paper clip, pine, white wallpaper

Private Collection

(Right)
Work Box

Alfred, ME

Early to mid-20th century

Height: 2"
Length: 5¾"
Width: 4"

Woven poplar and sweet grass, green satin silk, green ribbon, kidskin, pearl button, paper clip, elastic, white wallpaper, pine, Alfred stamp. Fitted with emery, wax, needle book, pincushion

Private Collection

CHAPTER

2

❦ Poplarware

Mount Lebanon, NY

*Sabbathday Lake and
Alfred, ME*

Canterbury and Enfield, NH

Assorted Poplarware

50. Handkerchief Boxes

(Rear)
Cardboard Box

Canterbury, NH

Mid-20th century

Height: 2¾"
Base: 5¾" square

Cardboard, inscribed on top, "Manufactured by the/Canterbury/Shakers/East Canterbury,/New Hampshire"

Private Collection

(Left)
Handkerchief Box

Canterbury, NH

Mid-20th century

Height: 2½"
Base: 4¼" square

Woven poplar, bright red moire fabric, kidskin, ribbon, elastic, shoe button, paper clip fastener, pine, tacks, yellow/green/orange wallpaper

Private Collection

(Right)
Handkerchief Box

Canterbury, NH

Mid-20th century

Height: 3"
Base: 5¼" square

Woven poplar, blue/white/gray striped cotton, kidskin, ribbon, shank button with metal clip, copper tacks, pine, blue/gray/white striped wallpaper

Private Collection

During the 1890s the Maine Shakers taught the poplar craft to the Canterbury, New Hampshire, community. At first, Canterbury bought their poplar cloth from Sabbathday Lake, but by 1928 they had purchased equipment from the Mount Lebanon, New York, community to plane and strip the poplar themselves. While New Hampshire poplarware never achieved the intricacy of the boxes made in Maine, the Canterbury Shakers found a ready market for their products.

Like the other communities, Canterbury marketed their fancy goods in many ways. They published at least five catalogs and had a fancy goods store at the village. They also traveled extensively to sell their wares, going to Florida, the Poconos, and the Carolinas, as well as the Atlantic coast and White Mountain resorts.

a. Style

The Handkerchief Box, a style very popular at Canterbury, was manufactured in six sizes, two of which are shown here.

b. Weave

The weave of the cloth on both of these boxes is the same as that used by the Sabbathday Lake Shakers. The material used in this cloth is natural poplar, but in earlier years the Canterbury Shakers were known to have used poplar, straw, and sweet grass in both natural and dyed colors.

c. Ribbons

The Canterbury Shakers usually tied the ribbons on their poplar boxes with one loop. On the tall box the choice of wider ribbons balances the height of the box.

d. Buttons

While they used a variety of buttons, the shank button with the metal center used on the larger box is common on Canterbury boxes. There are always exceptions, however, and the button on the open box is a shoe button.

d. Rear closing

About the time Eldress Bertha Lindsay took charge of the industry at Canterbury (1943-1958), the overlapping closure of the poplar strip on the body of the box was moved from the center back of the box to a rear corner. This gave the back of the box the uninterrupted line, which can be seen in the open box.

e. Cardboard box

The Shakers admired the poplar cloth's natural white color, but the cloth darkened with exposure to light. Handkerchief Boxes were often packed in cardboard boxes for protection against both light and wear. This box is one of several styles and sizes made. A piece of fabric was attached to the outside of the box to indicate the color of the box within.

51. Two Later Containers

The Jewelry Box and Card Tray, along with the popular Handkerchief Box, were made in the largest numbers by the Canterbury, New Hampshire, Shakers from the 1930s onward. The Card Tray was produced in three sizes.

a. Materials
By the mid-19th century, high quality materials needed for the poplarware were becoming difficult to obtain. As the number of community members dwindled, shopping trips to Boston and New York became more difficult. In 1958, Canterbury closed its industry. The later poplar pieces show the compromises in materials that were made. The lining of the Jewelry Box is a printed cotton fabric instead of the satin or velvet used previously.

b. Kidskin
High quality kidskin for the poplarware was one of the most difficult materials for the Shakers to obtain. Poor kidskin was too thick, giving the trim a heavier look as a consequence. The thick kidskin used on the scalloped top does not readily stretch over the undulating edge, creating noticeable wrinkles.

c. Tacks
Over time, oxidation on copper tacks used to nail the cardboard strip to the wooden base bled through the kidskin trim. When available, brass escutcheon pins were used to avoid this problem.

d. Wallpaper base
The Canterbury community used heavily patterned wallpapers to cover the bases of their poplar boxes. This came from extra wallpaper used in village papering projects, and from free wallpaper sample books obtained in local stores.

e. Canterbury Stamp

(Top)
Jewelry Box

Canterbury, NH

Mid-20th century

Height: 1¾"
Length: 4¼"
Width: 2⅝"

Woven poplar, blue cotton fabric with bright pink and lavender flowers, lavender ribbon, kidskin, shank button with metal clip, elastic, pine, tacks, patterned wallpaper

Private Collection

(Bottom)
Card Tray

Canterbury, NH

Early to mid-20th century

Height: 1¾"
Length: 7"
Width: 4½"

Woven poplar, green satin silk, kidskin, green ribbon, pine, tacks, patterned wallpaper

Private Collection

52. Handkerchief Box

The Enfield, New Hampshire, community does not appear to have had as large a poplarware industry as the Canterbury, New Hampshire, and the Maine communities, judging from the quantity of boxes extant today. Well-made examples of boxes from this community can, however, be found.

a. Material

Straw often appears in Enfield, New Hampshire, boxes. The outer surface of straw is very shiny, while the inside is dull; and the Shakers used both sides of the straw to achieve special effects in their weave. A magnifying lens is often useful to determine the materials used in a box. While reversed straw looks very much like poplar, poplar can be identified by its wood grain. Straw cloth was used in many Shaker communities for bonnets, and it was either woven plain or with poplar added, or woven alternating the shiny and dull sides, as in this box.

b. Condition

Notwithstanding its worn condition, this box has many good features. The workmanship is excellent, the box is stamped, and the materials and weaving pattern set it apart from more common boxes. This box can be valued as a good example of the community's work.

c. Base

The base is covered with plain white paper and marked with the community's stamp: "FROM THE SHAKERS,/ENFIELD, N.H.".

d. Enfield Stamp

Enfield, NH

Early to mid-19th century

Height: 2½"
Base: 4¾" square

Woven straw, green satin silk, kidskin, velvet ribbon, pearl button, paper clip, elastic, pine, tacks, white wallpaper, Enfield stamp

Private Collection

❧ **Poplarware**

Work Boxes
(see color plate 7 on page 23)

Ladies' Work Basket
Canterbury, NH
Woven poplar, blue silk satin, kidskin, blue ribbon, elastic, shank button with clip, pine, tacks, blue striped wallpaper, written in pencil on base: "Shakers/Canterbury/New Hamp.". fitted with pincushion, emery, wax

Work Casket
Alfred, ME
Woven poplar and sweet grass, pine frame and base, kidskin, pink ribbon, velvet, pearl buttons, cane, velvet, wallpaper. Fitted with emery, needle book, and wax

Square Work Box
Church Family, Mt. Lebanon, NY
Woven poplar, white embossed paper, yellow ribbons, cane, pine frame. Fitted with pincushion, emery, and wax

a. Weave
These boxes reveal a variety of weaving patterns that can be found on poplar boxes. The Work Casket makes use of two weaves: the plain Alfred, Maine, weave on the body, and the more decorative weave incorporating sweet grass on the pocket. The Ladies' Work Basket illustrates the typical weave found on many Maine and New Hampshire boxes. The Square Work Box is covered with the flat weave frequently used on Mount Lebanon, New York, boxes.

b. Color
The head of the industry in each community selected the fabrics to be used in their poplarware. These fabrics range from the vividly colored linings and ribbons of the two upper boxes to the pastel shades in the Work Casket. The Canterbury, New Hampshire, Shakers noted in their catalogs that poplar goods were available in eight "standard" colors: blue, pink, red, green, yellow, corn, lavender, and purple.

c. Ladies' Work Basket
The Canterbury Shakers sold Ladies' Work Baskets in oblong and octagonal shapes. This is the largest oblong size, #0, which sold for $5.00 and was the most expensive poplar item in the Canterbury catalog. While there are four bows on the outside of this box, the interior is fitted with only a pincushion, emery, and cupcake-shaped wax. Needle books were not included, and were sold separately.

Striped Boxes

(see color plate 8 on page 24)

Work Box
Possibly Canterbury, NH
Dyed and natural woven poplar, green satin silk, green ribbon, kidskin, elastic, pearl button, tacks, wallpaper. Fitted with pincushion, wax, emery, needle book

Handkerchief Box
Community unknown
Dyed and natural woven straw, pink satin silk, pink ribbon, kidskin, elastic, purple glass button, clip, pine, tacks, white wallpaper

Open Work Box
Community unknown
Dyed and natural woven straw, yellow satin silk, kidskin, copper tacks, cane, yellow ribbon, pine, patterned silver wallpaper, tacks. Fitted with pincushion, emery, needle book

Handkerchief Box
Community unknown
Dyed and natural woven straw, lavender satin silk, purple glass button, straight pin, lavender ribbons, kidskin, elastic, pine, tacks, patterned white wallpaper

These four boxes illustrate a category of boxes found on the market today that as yet cannot be definitely linked to a community of origin. While they are similar in shape to the proceeding boxes, the striking use of dyed materials sets them apart.

a. Materials
Straw, both natural and dyed, is used for the two Handkerchief Boxes and the Open Work Box, while the Sewing Basket is completely made of poplar, both natural and dyed. The strips of straw used in the two Handkerchief Boxes are much narrower than the ordinary ¹⁄₁₆" width poplar used in the Work Box.

b. Weave
The weaving pattern is different on each of these boxes. These patterns and the addition of dyed materials makes these boxes very striking.

c. Ribbons
The ribbons on the larger Handkerchief Box are unusual. Instead of the usual single ribbon tied in a loop, there are two ribbons, one tied in a double bow on top of which is another ribbon tied in a single bow.

d. Similarities
The two Handkerchief Boxes have some features in common. The stripes on the lids run from front to rear, unlike the more common side to side stripe seen on the Sewing Basket. Both boxes have purple glass buttons, which might suggest they were made in the same community.

53. Poplar Smalls

Many of the small poplar items assembled in this photograph can be found on the market today. This is a collection of small sewing items made from poplar cloth that can be found in a broad range of weaves, shapes, and sizes. Community identification of these smalls is more difficult unless they are found attached to the interior of a poplar box from a known community. The Shakers made a large variety of Needle Books and Basket Cushions that were sold separately from boxes.

a. Basket Cushions
At the top are four round Basket Cushions and one square one. Basket Cushions, as distinguished from pincushions, sat in poplar containers that have either plain or scalloped tops. The velvet pincushions were either embroidered in a "tomato" pattern seen in the top four Basket Cushions, or left plain like the square Sabbathday Lake pincushion. "Tomato" pincushions were also available separately, made in a variety of sizes in either satin or cashmere.

b. Trays
A variety of small trays were made to hold calling cards or small notions. They can be found in round, rectangular, or diamond shapes. The scalloped edge box (center) is a finely made tray from Sabbathday Lake, Maine.

c. Needle books
Needle Books vary in material, weave, and shape. A common form was the simple book with flannel "pages" seen to the right of the Tray. At other times, this needle book was attached to a velvet pincushion, such as the one from Mount Lebanon, New York, seen in front of the square pincushion. The needle book here is closed with a ribbon at the bottom. The Pinflat (lower left) is made by sandwiching a velvet pincushion between two pieces of plain poplar wood.

d. Handkerchief Case
The flat square on the right is a Handkerchief Case, made from two pieces of lined poplar cloth held together by elastic. Folded hand-kerchiefs were slipped inside the two layers of poplar. These can also be found covered with kidskin instead of poplar.

54. End of the Trade Boxes

By the mid-20th century poplar cloth
and other materials, such as buttons
and fine fabrics, were becoming
difficult to acquire, and the two
remaining Shaker communities,
Sabbathday Lake, Maine, and
Canterbury, New Hampshire, made
different choices affecting their poplar
industries. Canterbury decided to close
its industry entirely, while Sabbathday
Lake chose to continue, but to change
their box coverings from poplar cloth
to other fabrics.

These two hexagon boxes show how the
poplar business evolved at Sabbathday
Lake, Maine. In 1942 the community
closed their Great Mill (1853), where the
poplar had been processed, but there
was enough poplar cloth on hand to
last until the 1950s. When it was
evident there would be no more poplar,
this community began to use other
materials, such as the upholstery and
leatherette in these boxes. The button
on the leatherette box is painted pink to
match the ribbons.

(Top)
Work Box

Sabbathday Lake, ME

Mid-20th century

Height: 2⅛"
Base: 4⅜"

*White upholstery fabric, red
satin silk, red ribbon,
kidskin, elastic, shoe button,
paper clip, tacks, pine, white
wallpaper, Sabbathday Lake
stamp. Fitted with flannel
needle book, red emery, pin
cushion, wax*

(Bottom)
Work Box

Sabbathday Lake, ME

Mid-20th century

Height: 2⅛"
Base: 4⅜"

*White leatherette, pink
cotton with floral pattern,
pink ribbon, kidskin, shoe
button, shank clip, pine,
tacks, white wallpaper.
Fitted with needle book,
emery, pincushion, wax*

3

❧ Questions and Answers
for Collectors

What's Shaker and What's Not: Questions and Answers for Collectors

How do you go about finding a Shaker basket or an item of poplarware?

It's much more difficult today than it was a few years ago, but many good examples are still available at reasonable cost, at least when compared to the availability and cost of Shaker furniture.

The quickest way is to consult a dealer who specializes in Shaker. But don't be surprised if the dealer has a waiting list of customers and collectors. Another possibility is a specialized Shaker auction. The caution here is that this may be your most expensive option. The least expensive market is, of course, a tag sale or a flea market. Although it may take years to turn up a treasure, the thrill of finding a genuine Shaker article amidst the clutter of a flea market will make the hard work worthwhile.

Many Shaker baskets and poplarware items are still undiscovered: a basket hanging in a barn perhaps, or a poplar box packed away long ago in someone's attic. It's our hope that this field guide will lead to the discovery of some neglected masterpieces, one day to be included in a future field guide or book.

As more examples emerge, our knowledge of baskets and poplarware will grow, and with it, these products from Shaker hands will secure their place as some of the finest and most desirable of all American craftware.

55. Round Basket

This is an apt example of "possibly Shaker," although the basket's exact provenance has not been established. Its shape and the fineness of its evenly cut splint suggests the hand of a Shaker basketmaker. Its unusual double-grip handles were made from woodsplint bent to shape. Its maker incorporated a lavender-colored ribbon in the bottom weave of the basket. The basket is decorated with a crocheted thimble holder attached to its handle.

What are the origins of Shaker basketry?

Shaker basketry has its origins in the rich and distinct traditions of New England splint basketmaking which includes, of course, the basketware of the Northeast American Indian tribes.

In the early 19th century when the Shakers began to "gather together" into their agricultural communities, baskets nothing much more than containers— were a necessity for their fields, barns, workshops, and dwellings. And like most early immigrants from Europe, many surely brought from their homelands practical basketmaking skills.

Probably Canterbury, NH

Height: 3¼"
Diameter: 7½"
Overall Height: 4"

Canterbury Village, Inc.
72.315.8

What is the influence of Native American basketmaking?

Although the forms of baskets, and the materials of construction, are seemingly infinite in their variety, most baskets are constructed by one of three weaving techniques: by plaiting, twining, or coiling.

In the 18th century basketmaking by the Native American tribes of the Northeast took a new direction away from twined and coiled basketry, and storage containers made from pieces of tree bark stitched together. Their new direction was the manufacture of basketware from plaited woodsplint. The same technique was used for most Shaker baskets. Plaited baskets are woven in a pattern in which a horizontal woodsplint element (the weft) passes over and under one or more vertical woodsplint elements (the waft). Precisely when this happened is an ongoing challenge to archaeologists and Native American historians.

Also missing in today's historical record is the reason why these Northeast Indians turned to plaited woodsplint basketry. Most likely it was the phenomenon of acculturation: the market for baskets in colonial America was vast and growing, forests of raw material were freely available, and plaited baskets could be manufactured in a fraction of the time required for coiled and twined basketry. Also, European-style basket shapes could be replicated by plaited-weave techniques, training was available from European missionaries, and the colonists' metal tools eased substantially the manual labor that goes into transforming a tree into ribbons of woodsplint.

These new Native American baskets were made primarily from the wood of the Black Ash tree (Fraxinus Nigra), a hardwood that thrived in the wetlands of New England and Canada. They were primarily storage baskets for tribal use, sale to the colonists, and eventually for the tourist market.

The Northeast Indians sold thousands, if not millions, of their baskets. Most antique baskets found today in New England are of Native American manu-facture. They are invariably made of black ash, and square, rectangular, or oval in shape.

To process the black ash, the Native Americans first removed the bark from a log of freshly cut black ash. The log was then pounded repeatedly, its full length, with a wooden mallet. This pounding separated the tree's annual growth rings, one or two years' growth at a time. The result is "splint," which the Native Americans pulled off the log lengthwise. The pounding process was then repeated to remove successive lawyers of growth ring.

These lengths of splint (the thickness of a nickel) were then lanced halfway through, along the grain. Each half was pulled apart to reveal a natural satin-like finish on the interior of each piece of splint. The splint was then cut into ribbon-like strips, or weavers, and woven into a basket, with the satin finish of the splint facing outward.

Can Shaker and Native American baskets be confused?

Because Shaker manufacture of baskets has roots in these Native American materials and processes, there are many similarities between their baskets. This has resulted in many baskets being mislabeled Shaker, or with the notorious "possibly Shaker," when in fact they are plainly Native American.

56. Northeast Indian Basket Rims

Baskets manufactured by the Northeast Indians are frequently confused with Shaker basketware. The use by both of black ash woodsplint and plaited weaving techniques contributes to the notorious and hedged misattribution—"possibly Shaker."

To the trained eye, however, Native American-made baskets are not difficult to identify. One of the more obvious differences is the absence of a carved outer rim on most Native American basketware. Instead, Native American basketmakers generally used a heavy piece of flat woodsplint, or annual growth ring.

Handles and rims on Native American baskets were usually split from unseasoned hardwood, hand-carved with a knife, and hand-bent to shape. As a result, they frequently lack the attention to detail that is characteristic of most Shaker basketware.

Another distinctive detail on Native American basketware is the handle with a single notch for the basket's rim. That single notch for the bottom of the rim is generally triangular in shape.

Adding to the confusion is the fact that many Native American baskets are in the collections of many Shaker communities. However, the final resting place of an artifact is no proof of its provenance. The Shakers maintained cordial social and economic relations with their Native American neighbors. Indeed, in Victorian America they were fierce business competitors for the tourist trade. Moveover, it was not uncommon for the Shakers to buy Native American baskets for community use, and for sale to the World's People when Shaker inventories dwindled.

Fruitlands Museum,
Harvard, MA
492.1980

57. Three Baskets

These are examples of fine baskets that can be found in collections of Shaker communities and that are frequently confused with Shaker basketware.

The plaited basket (front), from the Hancock Shaker Village collection, is of Northeast Indian manufacture. It was made from wide black ash woodsplint, and is decorated with round and square blockprints. Typical of Native American baskets, the flat outer rim was made from woodsplint; that is, annual growth ring.

The hamper basket (right) is made of white willow. It's a German import. The Shakers purchased them in great quantities for resale to the World's People, sometimes with Shaker-added decorations. Many surviving examples can be traced to specific Shaker communities, but they were not made by the Shakers. This example is in the Hancock Shaker Museum collection.

The black ash basket (left), from a private collection, is popularly called a "Taconic," or "Bushwacker" basket. These sturdy baskets, typically round in shape, were made by families of basketmakers residing in the hills of Columbia County in New York State. They used heavyweight woodsplint from black ash, maple, and oak. Bushwacker baskets have distinctive hand-carved rims and ear-shaped handles.

Lack of documentation makes it difficult, even for experts, to identify the exact provenance of specific baskets, or their community of manufacture. Ironically, the Shakers themselves have made this task of identification extremely difficult by their tradition of gifting baskets between members of the separate communities; by their purchase and sale of Native American and European imports; by the sharing of prefabricated handles and rims among communities; and by the closing of active villages and the transfer of existing members and property to other Shaker communities.

Nonetheless, some records categorically prove pedigree. There are also distinct styles and manufacturing techniques that permit a confident identification of many baskets as being Shaker-made, or to be linked to specific Shaker communities. The task is easiest with utility baskets, and extremely difficult in the case of fancy work baskets because of their identical designs and techniques of manufacture.

Private Collection

Hancock Shaker Village
Pittsfield, MA
72.315.27; 79.39

Are there other baskets that can be mistaken for Shaker?

Basketmaking was not, of course, exclusively the craft of the Native Americans and Shakers. There have always been professional basketmakers. And it was probably the rare farmer who did not make incidental baskets for domestic and farm use. Woods used include the black ash, white ash, split oak, and maple. The farmer's baskets may reveal a crude hand, but they served his purpose well.

How can I determine if a piece is really poplar?

Because some pieces on the market are mistakenly labeled as poplar, some suggestions follow to help in an initial evaluation of any poplar piece being considered. Carefully examine the texture and the weave of the material against the pictures in this book to determine if it is indeed poplar. The photographs in the text will illustrate the materials the Shakers used in their poplar boxes: strips of poplar wood, at times interwoven with natural and dyed ash, straw, or sweet grass.

Note the color of the cloth. Poplar cloth darkens with age. Even well preserved pieces take on a yellow hue. Beale & Gibbs are the only crafts people reproducing poplar in volume today. The white color of the new poplar cloth items is readily apparent in their boxes; however, each of their poplar items is clearly numbered and stamped "Beale and Gibbs."

Check for repairs. Look for original ribbons, which although faded, should match the interior fabric. Repaired kidskin is often much whiter and thicker than the original.

Look for a community stamp on the base; often there is one.

Note the condition of the box. Poplar is fragile and a little wear is to be expected if the box has been used. Damaged pieces, however, lose their value.

58. Three Doll's Bonnets

Doll's bonnets were a popular sales items in gifts shops in all Shaker villages. They were sold either on dressed dolls or separately. The dolls were made in several sizes in a variety of dress. The center bonnet is from a doll known to have been dressed by Sister Mary Dahm of the Watervliet, New York, community.

At Mount Lebanon, the Church Family sold doll's sun bonnets made from straw in six sizes.

The 20th century bonnets seen here are made of poplar and straw. Bonnets sold in communities like Harvard, Massachusetts, and Watervliet, New York, that were not known to have produced poplar cloth, were probably made from cloth purchased from other communities such as Mount Lebanon or Sabbathday Lake, and then assembled in these villages.

Doll's bonnets are often represented on the market today as poplar. The smallest bonnet (center) is woven straw, which can be identified by its shiny appearance in comparison to the others. The largest bonnet is made of a cloth woven with straw and poplar. The cloth of the bonnet on the left is completely poplar cloth and its finish, when compared to the other bonnets, appears dull.

(Top left)
Doll's Bonnet

Community Unknown

*Late 19th - early 20th
century*

Height: 3"

*Woven poplar, blue satin
silk, kidskin*

Private Collection

(Top right)
Doll's Bonnet

Community unknown

20th century

*Woven straw and poplar,
red satin silk, kidskin*

*The Shaker Museum,
Old Chatham, NY
8167*

(Center)
Doll's Bonnet

Watervliet, NY

20th century

*Woven straw, satin silk,
kidskin*

*The Shaker Museum,
Old Chatham, NY
19259*

59. Two Palm Leaf Containers

Containers like these are found on the market in a wide variety of shapes and sizes and are often described as Shaker-made. The Shakers did use palm leaf in several of their products, such as bonnets and fans. These Victorian containers, however, were definitely not made by the Shakers. As yet, no documentation has come to light to explain their origin, whether imported or domestic. The decoration is "superfluous" even by the standards of the Shakers of the Victorian era. The market value of these palm leaf boxes is not comparable to the market value of genuine Shaker poplar boxes.

How can I determine if a piece is authentic Shaker?

One of the purposes of this Field Guide is help collectors, students of Shaker crafts, and contemporary basketmakers to identify the real thing. Heretofore, the most honest answer to the question, "How can you tell if it's authentic Shaker?" has been the unsatisfying, "You really have to see the real thing, over and over." The assembly of the rich variety of Shaker artifacts for this Field Guide has been, in effect, a search for a better answer.

(Top)
Handkerchief Box

Non-Shaker

Late 19th - early 20th century

Height: 2¼"
Length: 6"
Width: 5½"

Palm leaf, reed, blue ribbon, elastic, wire, cardboard

Private Collection

(Bottom)
Glove Box

Non-Shaker

20th Century

Height: 1⅜"
Length: 9½"

Palm leaf, reed, isinglass, paint, ribbon

Private Collection

CHAPTER

4

❦ Shaker Communities
Then and Now

Chronology of Important
Shaker Dates

Bibliography

Index

About the Authors

Shaker Communities Then and Now

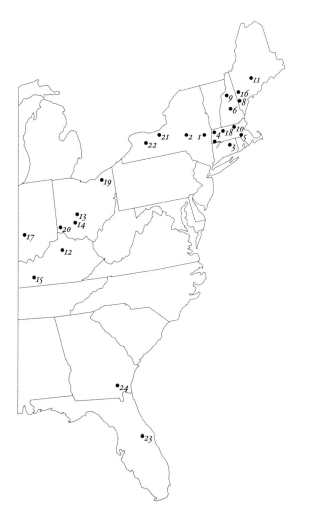

1   *New Lebanon, NY*
     (1787-1947) ••

2   *Watervliet, NY*
     (1787-1938) ••

3   *Enfield, CT*
     (1790-1917) •••

4   *Hancock, MA*
     (1790-1960) ••

5   *Harvard, MA*
     (1791-1918) •••

6   *Canterbury, NH*
     (1792-1992) ••

7   *Tyringham, MA*
     (1792-1875) •••

8   *Alfred, ME*
     (1793-1931) •••

9   *Enfield, NH*
     (1793-1923) ••

10   *Shirley, MA*
     (1793-1908) •••

11   *Sabbathday Lake, ME*
     (1794-present) •

12   *Pleasant Hill, KY*
     (1814-1910) ••

13   *Union Village, OH*
     (1812-1910) •••

Chronology of
Important Dates

14 *Watervliet, OH*
    (1806-1900) •••

15 *South Union, KY*
    (1807-1922) ••

16 *Gorham, ME*
    (1808-1819) •••

17 *West Union, IN*
    (1810-1827) •••

18 *Savoy, MA*
    (1817-1825) •••

19 *North Union, OH*
    (1822-1889) •••

20 *Whitewater, OH*
    (1824-1907) •••

21 *Sodus, NY*
    (1826-1936) •••

22 *Groveland, NY*
    (1836-1892) •••

23 *Narcoossee, FL*
    (1896-1911) •••

24 *White Oak, GA*
    (1898-1902) •••

•   *Existing community*

•• *Restored buildings or museum*

••• *Former community*

1736 *Ann Lee is born in Manchester, England*

1758 *Ann Lee joins the "Shaking Quakers."*

1774 *Ann Lee and eight followers come to America.*

1776 *First Shaker settlement at Niskayuna, New York.*

1780 *The Shakers "open the gospel" and seek converts; Joseph Meacham joins the Shakers.*

1784 *Mother Ann dies.*

1785 *First meetinghouse built at New Lebanon, New York.*

1794 *By this date eleven villages established "in gospel order."*

1805 *Three Shaker missionaries travel to Kentucky.*

1806 *First western society established at Pleasant Hill, Kentucky.*

1837 *Visions of four girls at Watervliet mark beginning of "Mother Ann's Work."*

1840-50 *Membership peaks at about four to six thousand.*

1905 *International Peace Conference at Mount Lebanon, New York.*

1920 *Only eight villages remain open.*

1959 *Hancock, Massachusetts closes; two villages remain open.*

1992 *Last Shaker at Canterbury dies*

1992 *Sabbathday Lake last remaining active Shaker community*

Selected Bibliography

Andrews, Edward Deming. *The Community Industries of the Shakers.* Albany: The University of the State of New York, 1932.

Andrews, Edward Deming. *The People Called Shakers: A Search for the Perfect Society.* New York: Oxford University Press, 1953.

Andrews, Edward Demming, and Faith Andrews. *Work and Worship Among the Shakers.* New York: Dover Publications, Inc., 1974.

Anonymous. *"Catalog of Goods Manufactured by the Canterbury Shakers."* The Shaker Museum, Old Chatham, NY, no. 249.

Anonymous. *"Catalog of Fancy Goods made at Shaker Village, Alfred, York County, Maine, 1908."* Reprint, Hands to Work Series, No. 1, The United Society of Shakers, Sabbathday Lake, ME, 1986.

Anonymous. *"Catalog of Fancy Goods Made by the Shakers, Sabbathday Lake, Maine, 1910."* United Society of Shakers, Sabbathday Lake, ME, 1992.

Anonymous. *"Hart & Shepard, Canterbury Shakers, Manufacturers of "Dorothy" Cloaks, Men's All-Wool Sweaters, Fancy Goods and Medicines. Hart & Shepard, East Canterbury. N. H."* The Shaker Museum, Old Chatham, NY, nos. 247, 244, 246.

Anonymous. *"Hart & Shepard, Manufacturers of Athletic and Fancy Goods, Holiday Goods a Specialty. Shakers, East Canterbury, N. H."* The Shaker Museum, Old Chatham, NY, 245.

Anonymous. *"Price List of Goods Manufactured And For Sale by the Shakers, Prudence Stickney, Sabbathday Lake, Maine."* n.d.

Anonymous. *"Price List of Goods Manufactured And For Sale by The Shakers, Sabbathday Lake, Maine."* n.d.

Anonymous. *"Products of Intelligence and Diligence", Shaker's Church Family, Mount Lebanon, Col. Co., New York."* Hancock Shaker Village, Hancock, MA.

Avery, Giles. *Records Kept by the Order of the Church, Vol III, 1856-1871.* The Shaker Museum, Old Chatham, NY (9757/10,342).

Avery, Giles. *Mt. Lebanon Records of the Church 1871-1905, kept by Giles Avery, Vol IV.* The Shaker Museum, Old Chatham, NY, (9757/10,343).

Blinn, C. Henry. *A Historical Record of the Society of Believers in Canterbury, N.H. (1792-1848)* Shaker Village Inc., Canterbury, NH.

Boswell, Mary Rose. *"Blessed In The Basket: An Exhibition of Shaker Containers at Canterbury N. H."* 1985.

Boswell, Mary Rose. *"The Manufacture of Poplar Cloth Boxes by the Shakers at Canterbury N.H."* Unpublished manuscript.

Index

Field Guides to Collecting Shaker Antiques

Shaker Woodenware, Vol. I – Boxes, carriers, buckets, dippers, sieves, pails, and tubs.

Shaker Woodenware, Vol. II – Woodworking tools, textile tools, kitchen utensils, and farm tools.

Shaker Baskets and Poplarware – Mount Lebanon production baskets, Canterbury baskets, baskets from other communities, early and transitional poplarware, and other poplarware.

Shaker Furniture

Shaker Iron, Tin, and Brass

Shaker Textiles, Costume, and Fancy Goods

Shaker Paper

Other Books on the Shakers Published by Berkshire House / Berkshire Traveller Press

By Ejner Handberg
Foreword by June Sprigg

Shop Drawings of Shaker Furniture and Woodenware,
Volumes 1, 2, 3

Shop Drawings of Shaker Iron and Tinware
(Spring 1993)

Measured Drawings of Shaker Furniture and Woodenware

About the Authors

Gerrie Kennedy of Worthington, Massachusetts, has been resident basket maker at Hancock Shaker Village since 1988. She is a contributing author of *Simple Gifts and Natural Baskets* (Storey Publishing), and gives classes and lectures about baskets and basketmaking at museums and schools throughout the East Coast.

Galen Beale of Loudon, New Hampshire, is co-author with Mary Rose Boswell of *The Earth Shall Blossom: Shaker Herbs and Gardening* (Countryman Press) and a contributing author of *Simple Gifts* (Storey). She learned to make poplarware from Canterbury Shaker Eldresses Bertha Lindsay and Gertrude Soule. She is currently a partner in Beale & Gibbs, makers of reproduction Shaker poplarware.

Jim Johnson heads a communications and design firm in Great Barrington, Massachusetts, and is a consultant and dealer in Shaker antiques. He is co-author with June Sprigg of *Colonial: Design in the New World* and *Shaker Woodenware, I and II.*

Paul Rocheleau, principal photographer, has been published in numerous magazines, including *Architectural Digest, Antiques World, Americana, American Craft,* and *Antiques Magazine.* His photography was featured in the catalogue of the 1986 exhibit, "Shaker Design" at the Whitney Museum of American Art. His books include *Shaker Design, O Appalachia,* and the New England editions of the *Smithsonian Guide to Historic America.*

Editor: Cia Elkin

Design: Norman Hulme, Art Director
    Robin Clark, Designer
    Mischke/Johnson & Company

Typeface: Adobe Garamond

Production Services: Ripinsky & Company